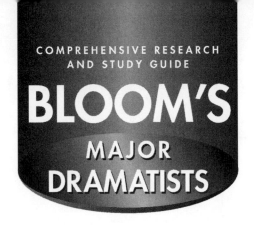

COMPREHENSIVE RESEARCH
AND STUDY GUIDE

BLOOM'S

MAJOR

DRAMATISTS

Luigi Pirandello

EDITED AND WITH AN
INTRODUCTION BY HAROLD BLOOM

CURRENTLY AVAILABLE

BLOOM'S MAJOR DRAMATISTS

Aeschylus
Aristophanes
Bertolt Brecht
Anton Chekhov
Euripides
Henrik Ibsen
Eugène Ionesco
Ben Jonson
Christopher Marlowe
Arthur Miller
Molière
Eugene O'Neill
Luigi Pirandello
Shakespeare's Comedies
Shakespeare's Histories
Shakespeare's Romances
Shakespeare's Tragedies
George Bernard Shaw
Sam Shepard
Neil Simon
Sophocles
Tom Stoppard
Oscar Wilde
Thornton Wilder
Tennessee Williams
August Wilson

COMPREHENSIVE RESEARCH
AND STUDY GUIDE

BLOOM'S

MAJOR
DRAMATISTS

Luigi Pirandello

EDITED AND WITH AN INTRODUCTION
BY HAROLD BLOOM

CHELSEA HOUSE
PUBLISHERS
A Haights Cross Communications Company
Philadelphia

© 2003 by Chelsea House Publishers, a subsidiary of
Haights Cross Communications.

A Haights Cross Communications ✦ Company

Introduction © 2003 by Harold Bloom.

Printed and bound in the United States of America.

First Printing
1 3 5 7 9 8 6 4 2

Library of Congress Cataloging-in-Publication Data
Luigi Pirandello / edited and with an introduction by Harold Bloom.
    p. cm. —(Bloom's major dramatists)
Includes bibliographical references and index.
  ISBN 0-7910-7036-0
  1. Pirandello, Luigi, 1867–1936—Criticism and interpretation. I.
Bloom, Harold. II. Series.
  PQ4835.I7 Z66487 2003
  852'.912—dc21

                                                        2002154040

Chelsea House Publishers
1974 Sproul Road, Suite 400
Broomall, PA 19008-0914

http://www.chelseahouse.com

Contributing Editor: Patsy Griffi

Cover design by Terry Mallon

Layout by EJB Publishing Services

CONTENTS

USER'S GUIDE

This volume is designed to present biographical, critical, and bibliographical information on the author and the author's best-known or most important plays. Following Harold Bloom's editor's note and introduction is a concise biography of the author that discusses major life events and important literary accomplishments. A critical analysis of each play follows, tracing significant themes, patterns, and motifs in the work. An annotated list of characters supplies brief information on the main characters in each play.

A selection of critical extracts, derived from previously published material, follows each thematic analysis. In most cases, these extracts represent the best analysis available from a number of leading critics. Because these extracts are derived from previously published material, they will include the original notations and references when available. Each extract is cited, and readers are encouraged to use the original publications as they continue their research. A bibliography of the author's writings, a list of additional books and articles on the author and their work, and an index of themes and ideas conclude the volume.

As with any study guide, this volume is designed as a supplement to the works being discussed, and is in no way intended as a replacement for those works. The reader is advised to read the text prior to using this study guide, and to keep it accessible for quick reference.

ABOUT THE EDITOR

Harold Bloom is Sterling Professor of the Humanities at Yale University and Henry W. and Albert A. Berg Professor of English at the New York University Graduate School. He is the author of over 20 books, and the editor of more than 30 anthologies of literary criticism.

Professor Bloom's works include *Shelley's Mythmaking* (1959), *The Visionary Company* (1961), *Blake's Apocalypse* (1963), *Yeats* (1970), *A Map of Misreading* (1975), *Kabbalah and Criticism* (1975), *Agon: Toward a Theory of Revisionism* (1982), *The American Religion* (1992), *The Western Canon* (1994), and *Omens of Millennium: The Gnosis of Angels, Dreams, and Resurrection* (1996). *The Anxiety of Influence* (1973) sets forth Professor Bloom's provocative theory of the literary relationships between the great writers and their predecessors. His most recent books include *Shakespeare: The Invention of the Human*, a 1998 National Book Award finalist, *How to Read and Why* (2000), and *Genius: A Mosaic of One Hundred Exemplary Creative Minds* (2002).

Professor Bloom earned his Ph.D. from Yale University in 1955 and has served on the Yale faculty since then. He is a 1985 MacArthur Foundation Award recipient and served as the Charles Eliot Norton Professor of Poetry at Harvard University in 1987–88. In 1999 he was awarded the prestigious American Academy of Arts and Letters Gold Medal for Criticism. Professor Bloom is the editor of several other Chelsea House series in literary criticism, including BLOOM'S MAJOR SHORT STORY WRITERS, BLOOM'S MAJOR NOVELISTS, BLOOM'S MAJOR DRAMATISTS, BLOOM'S MODERN CRITICAL INTERPRETATIONS, BLOOM'S MODERN CRITICAL VIEWS, and BLOOM'S BIOCRITIQUES.

EDITOR'S NOTE

My introduction ruminates upon how Pirandello's plays revive the ancient Sicilian art of sophistic rhetoric, which implicitly identifies psychology with figurative language. I apply this identification to the question of aesthetic dignity in *Henry IV*.

There are four "Critical Views" of *Right You Are (If You Think You Are)*, all of them useful. I particularly commend Jerome Mazzaro's insights into the play's narrator.

On *Six Characters in Search of an Author*, all six critical extracts are illuminating. I single out Anna Balakian who relates the play to Surrealism.

There are seven "Views" of Pirandello's masterwork, *Henry IV*. All have admirable aspects but central, in my judgement, are the observations of the dean of Pirandello critics, Eric Bentley. He analyzes *Henry IV* as a tragic farce and as a version of Pirandello's obsessive pattern in which the trivial or wicked characters seek the truth while the serious figures seek love, only to find that it has become impossible for them.

Tonight We Improvise has five critics represented, all of them again highly useful. The relationship of the play to *commedia dell'arte* is stressed both by Olga Ragusa and James Fisher.

Harold Bloom

Rhetoric, in its origins, was a Sicilian art, and it is fitting that the most rhetorical of modern dramatists, Luigi Pirandello, was also a Sicilian. The founder of rhetoric was the Sicilian shaman Empedocles, who preceded Plato in attempting to transform language from *doxa* (opinion) to truth, from the image-thinking of poetry to the concept-thinking of philosophy. Yet rhetoric stubbornly remained poetic, the instrument of a will-to-identity rather than a knower/known dualism. Gorgias, the Sicilian sophist who followed Empedocles, used rhetoric as Pirandello did, to enchant the audience into a realization of the antithetical nature of all truth. Plato, opposing this relativism, brought psychology and rhetoric overtly closer, but in essence they seem to me always one, with ancient and Renaissance cosmology making a third. In Pirandello, the Sicilian identity of rhetoric, psychology, and cosmology is confirmed. Though I agree with Eric Bentley, Pirandello's canonical critic, that the dramatist of *Henry IV* and *Six Characters in Search of an Author* is an Ibsenite, I find Pirandello closest to Gorgias. Pirandello is the playwright-as-sophist, leading us to the relativity of all truth, through an antithetical style.

An opportunistic perspectivism, *kairos*, is the occasion for the Pirandello drama as it was for the Gorgias oration. Bentley acutely notes the rhetoricity of Pirandello, which masks as an antirhetoric but is a stormy counter-rhetoric:

> His strongest weapon is his prose. Its torrential eloquence and pungent force are unique in the whole range of modern drama, and recall the Elizabethans (in contrast to our verse playwrights who imitate the Elizabethans and do not in the least recall them). He gets effects that one would not have thought possible to colloquial prose, thus compelling us to reopen the discussion of poetry and drama, in which it has always been assumed that prose was a limitation.

Bentley quotes Pirandello on his own achievement, in a passage that carries us back to ancient Sicily and Gorgias' insistence upon *kairos*, the opportune word for the opportune moment, here in Pirandello "the word that will be the action ... the living word ... the immediate expression." One wonders if there is an element in Sicilian culture, repressive and sublimely explosive, that guarantees this continuity with ancient rhetoric even as Pirandello expounds his idea of dramatic composition:

> So that the characters may leap from the written pages alive and self-propelled, the playwright needs to find the word that will be the action itself spoken, the living word that moves, the immediate expression, having the same nature as the act itself, the unique expression that cannot but be this—that is, appropriate to this given character in this given situation; words, expressions, which are not invented but are born, where the author has identified himself with his creature to the point of feeling as it feels itself, wishing it as it wishes itself.

An art this rhetorical carries us back to Jacobean drama, the closest modern equivalent of which I would locate in Pirandello's extraordinary *Henry IV* (1922), though Beckett's *Endgame* comes to mind as an even darker rival. If Pirandello's *Henry IV*, generally regarded as a tragical farce, is also to be granted the status of tragedy, of a modern *Hamlet*, it can only be if the representation of the nameless nobleman, Pirandello's protagonist, possesses the aesthetic dignity appropriate to tragic art. That dignity turns upon his rhetorical persuasiveness, since the nameless one *wants* to be a tragic hero. Bentley, with great shrewdness, notes that Pirandello is not persuaded by his own creature:

> The protagonist insists on tragedy; the author does not. The protagonist is a character in search of the tragic poet: such is Pirandello's subject, which therefore comes out absurd, grotesque, tragicomic.

Dialectically, Bentley is accurate, and I think he interprets the play as Pirandello wished it to be interpreted. But strong rhetoric resists our will-to-power when we seek to interpret it, and the nameless one is a powerful rhetorician. Bentley thinks him essentially mad and regards his final stabbing of Belcredi as a crime. Belcredi is a skeptic and a jokester; in the world of *Henry*

IV that marks him for death. Against such a view, Bentley argues that "this is not a tragedy, a heroic genre, but post-Dostoevski psychological drama showing the decline and fall of a man through mental sickness to crime." Time sustains Bentley, but then tragedy is no longer a heroic genre for us. It still is for the nameless one who has played at being Henry IV, and I am on his side as against Bentley and Pirandello, whose cruel joke it is that this character has found the wrong author at the wrong time.

That still leaves us with the puzzle of aesthetic dignity in *Henry IV*. The nameless one surely is in search of Kleist to serve as his author, or if he cannot get Kleist, he would take Schiller. Pirandello, the Sicilian sophist, has created an Idealist protagonist for his Materialist play, and I suspect that the nameless one stabs Bercredi as a substitute for Pirandello himself, for having failed to let himself become a Kleist or a Schiller. If the nameless one is our Hamlet, then Pirandello is our Claudius in this clash of mighty opposites. *Henry IV* becomes its protagonist's revenge upon Pirandello for refusing to write a tragedy rather than a farce. And yet the grand rhetoric of this Sicilian descendant of Empedocles and Gorgias takes a subtler and more beautiful revenge. Few moments in modern drama have the poignance of the vision Pirandello grants us of the nameless one and his inadequate retainers sitting together in the lamplight, with the marvelous antithesis of the actors, acting the part of acting Henry IV and his retainers, set against the rhetoric, at once ironic and opportunistic, of the nameless Idealist:

> HENRY IV: Ah, a little light! Sit there around the table, no, not like that; in an easy, elegant manner! ... (*To Harold.*) Yes, you, like that! (*Poses him.*) (*Then to Berthold.*) You, so! ... and I, here! (*Sits opposite them.*) We could do with a little decorative moonlight. It's very useful for us, the moonlight. I feel a real necessity for it, and pass a lot of time looking up at the moon from my window. Who would think, to look at her that she knows that eight hundred years have passed, and that I, seated at the window, cannot really be Henry IV gazing at the moon like any poor devil? But, look, look! See what a magnificent night scene we have here: the emperor surrounded by his faithful counselors! ... How do you like it?

How do we like it? Despite the overt irony, it seems too tragic for farce, but perhaps only for this single moment. Pirandello, in his counter-rhetoric, does remain an ancient Sicilian rhetorician and charms us into relativity by the incantation of his antitheses. His influence upon other dramatists came through his innovations as a counter-illusionist, but his continued influence upon us is rhetorical as well as dramatic.

BIOGRAPHY OF

Luigi Pirandello

Luigi Pirandello was born in 1867 in Girgenti (now Agrigento) on the island of Sicily to a prosperous sulpher dealer and his wife. Pirandello grew up in a provincial, rather feudal Sicilian society in the midst of a slow economic decline—a decline that facilitated the growth of the Mafiosi. Living in a close-knit, clannish community brought close scrutiny, and the more sensitive citizens, like Pirandello, lived in fear of calling attention to themselves. Pirandello's father, Stefano Pirandello, was a bold, impressive man who was secure in his wealth, which, in turn, provided security for Luigi. Yet his taciturn and severe disposition towards Luigi, left the son without any sense of being loved. Communication with his mother, Caterina Ricci-Gramitti, was awkward and strained at best.

Pirandello had expected to live a comfortable life, though his father expected him to become a businessman. His father's fortune gained from sulphur mining seemingly assured his future. At 19, after finishing the studies that he thought would direct his future career, he came home to work in the mines where he found the work to be unnatural, brutal, and exploitative. He then entered the University of Rome in 1887, but later transferred to Bonn University where he completed his doctoral thesis in Roman philology. Pirandello's literary efforts began in earnest with his translation of Goethe's *Roman Elegies*, and the publication of two collections of poetry and one collection of stories.

In 1894 Pirandello Married Antonietta Portulano, the daughter of his father's business partner. A fellow Sicilian, Antonietta also suffered from the distrusting and oppressive atmosphere in Sicily. Her father, a wretchedly jealous man, forced her to stifle all evidence of communication with men—a behavior that would later manifest into her own jealousies. In 1904, after the birth of their third child and the loss of the family fortune in a flood, Antonietta suffered a mental breakdown. Her violent paranoia lead her to believe that Pirandello committed sexual transgressions, and caused her to terrorize Pirandello and their three children. But paranoia has no restraints, and no censors for its envisioning of others' vile actions, and thus, like his parents, Pirandello's wife could not respond to his great need for talk and love.

Prior to his wife's breakdown, Pirandello had taken a position teaching Italian literature at the Normal College for Women in Rome where he taught for 24 years. When Pirandello's father lost his wealth, the family struggled financially on his teacher's salary. His first widely acclaimed novel *The Late Mattia Pascal* was written in 1904, after which he published two other novels and several short stories. In 1916 Pirandello turned his attention to the theater writing *Better Think Twice About It!*, *Liolà*, and *Right You Are (If You Think You Are)*.

In the eight years following, he wrote twenty-eight plays, some of which were stage adaptations of his earlier novels. Domestic drama became for him a venue for the literal staging of emotional problems, which his characters debate with themselves and in conversation with others. These personal themes helped Pirandello's plays connect with audiences in a way that plays may not have done since Shakespeare. They were not always immediately popular; *Six Characters in Search of an Author* caused a near riot in the audience after its first performance, but the next presentation received an enthusiastic response. Becoming familiar with Pirandello's plays may be said to have improved actors' performances, as well as audience behavior. Critics sometimes complained about a certain incomprehensible quality, but audiences were not as picayunish.

Interesting stage effects grew out of the Pirandellean resistance to the ordinary stage setting. In Paris, Pitoeff lowered the "six characters" in an elevator of sorts onto a stage awash in green lighting—the lighting for ghostly effects—in keeping with the theme that the characters cannot die in the playwright's mind because they have not yet lived on the stage and must torment him until they do. This production of *Six Characters* set the standard for Pirandello in the enormously positive audience response.

Pirandello created his own company and taught his actors the importance of entering the character, basing his instruction on Stanislavski's techniques. Passion that grew out of the character's nature became a norm. He stepped up the tempo of plays, so that they became more vital, more like improvisation. Indeed, he may be said to have brought life back to drama. He was himself a dynamic actor who believed in rigorous, short-term rehearsals and actors memorizing the lines of the plays, which they rarely did in Pirandello's time.

Finally, Pirandello's success could not have happened without Mussolini who, in a sense, replaced his father. Mussolini made possible Pirandello's National Art Theatre in Rome, which later toured the great cities. Pirandello's wife's confinement in 1919 freed him of her mental turmoil. She had long said that she wished to go away from him (to a clinic) and never return, and so she did until she died in the 1940s. Yet, paradoxically, her absence was so painful to him that he moved from where they had lived together. In 1934 Pirandello was awarded the Nobel Prize for Literature—he died two years later in 1936.

PLOT SUMMARY OF

Right You Are (If You Think You Are)

Right You Are (If You Think You Are) or *Così è, Se Vi Pare!* is presented as "A Parable in Three Acts." The play received its world premier in Milan in 1917, and was first published in 1918. The play's overarching discussion of the nature of the truth was especially poignant in Eric Bently's revival during the 1950s era of Macarthyism. Indeed the principle that emerges from the play's events is that the truth is not only elusive, but highly relative.

Right You Are takes place in "Our Own Times, in a Small Italian Town, the Capital of a Province." The story chronicles the community's overwhelming interest into the private lives of its newest inhabitants: Signor Ponza, his wife Signora Ponza, and his mother-in-law Signora Frola. The town's curiosity centers around the seemingly bizarre living situation for the Ponza's in which Signor Ponza has rented an upscale apartment for his mother-in-law while settling himself and his wife into a disreputable and run-down tenement. Further complicating the issue is the fact that Signor Ponza pays frequent visits to Signora Frola, but does not allow her to visit her daughter.

Act I opens in the parlor in the house of Commendatore Agazzi, a provincial councelor. Present are Agazzi, Amalia (Agazzi's wife and Laudisi's sister), Dina (Agazzi's daughter), and Lamberto Laudisi. Laudisi, the constant voice of reason, is described as "a man nearing the forties, quick and energetic in his movement," who is "smartly dressed" in good taste.

The action begins with Laudisi pacing up and down the parlor expressing his frustration that Agazzi has used his governmental position to lodge a complaint with Signor Ponza's superior (Ponza is another governmental official). It is revealed that Amalia and Dina called on Signora Frola, and were refused, thus instigating the complaint. While Amalia insists that they were only calling on Signora Frola as a courtesy, Dina suggests that it was more out of an unavoidable curiosity, arguing that the

Ponza's have intentionally peaked the town's interests. Dina then reveals that she and the rest of the town have been to see the tenement that Ponza has secured for him and his wife. She describes it as having "an interior court so dark at noontime you can hardly see your hand before your face." Furthermore, the Ponza apartment on the top floor has a basket by which the wife and mother-in-law communicate. When Laudisi suggests that it is not so odd for a son-in-law and a mother-in-law to not get along, Dina informs him that the two get along very well. For every defense Laudisi supplies, Amalia and Dina provide further evidence to suggest the impropriety of the Ponza's circumstances.

Signor Sirelli arrives with his wife and Signora Cini. Sirelli is also around forty years old, and he is described as being bald, fat, and overdressed. His wife is described as plump and "overdressed with the provincial's fondness for display;" she is a gossip, and her main concern is in keeping her husband in his proper place. Signora Cini takes delight in the failings of others, and is described as "the old provincial lady of affected manners." After introductions are made, Signora Sirelli states that their intended purpose is to seek truth about Mr. Ponza. During the course of discussion, Sirelli reveals that Ponza keeps his wife locked up at home.

Signor and Signora Sirelli bicker over the accuracy of the information Signor Sirelli provides, at which point Laudisi interjects that Sirelli can only present things as they appear to him, which must naturally seem accurate. Laudisi then has both Mr. And Mrs. Sirelli admit to seeing and touching him to prove that he exists. He then posits that while each person in the room sees him, they all see him differently, and most certainly they view him differently than he views himself. To this end, he concludes that it is futile to try to understand the truth behind the Ponza's living situation.

After Laudisi removes himself from the conversation, Amelia and Dina relate the story of how they were not received by Signora Frola. It is revealed here that signor Ponza answered the door, and much is made of his facial features, and the fact that he dresses in black. It is also revealed that they hail from a neighboring town that was destroyed by an earthquake. After the telling of how Signor Ponza answered the door with "the eyes of a devil," and how he expressed a general lack of courtesy, Commendatore Agazzi enters the room and announces that Signora Frola will arrive shortly.

Agazzi reports that the prefect, to whom he reported Ponza's strange behavior, took a great interest in what was being said, and agreed that the mystery should be cleared up stating, "as a matter of his own official prestige, for all this mystery in connection with one of his assistants to be cleared up, so that once and for all we shall know the truth." To this, Laudisi laughs.

Upon Signora Frola's entrance, pleasantries are exchanged, as she apologizes for having neglected her social obligations. When she ask the comendatore's pardon, he explains that he was quite put out by the affair. To this she responds with the story of the earthquake and how the family had suffered the loss of all of their relatives. Signora Sirelli questions the odd living arrangements, and Signora Frola explains that a young man and a young woman who are married should be left alone. At this point Laudisi re-enters the conversation agreeing whole-heartedly with Signora Frola.

Under heavy cross examination, Signora Frola explains her daughter's reclusiveness by stating that women from the country are used to staying indoors. She further explains that while she visits her daughter regularly, the five flights of stairs are too much for her to climb, so they meet courtyard to balcony. Under further questioning, Signora Frola delicately tries to explain that Signor Ponza prefers his wife to express her emotions for her mother through him. After trying to defend Signor Ponza's desires to keep his and his wife's love for each other uncompromised (even by the love of a mother), Signora Frola takes her leave.

After Signora Frola has left, the group expresses doubts concerning her explanations, and Signor Ponza arrives. He is described as:

a short, thick set, dark complexioned man of a distinctly unprepossessing appearance; black hair, very thick and coming down low over his forehead; a black mustache upcurling at the ends, giving his face a certain ferocity of expression. He is dressed entirely in black. From time to time he draws a black-bordered handkerchief and wipes the perspiration from his brow. When he speaks his eyes are invariably hard, fixed, sinister.

After being received, Ponza announces that he has something of a declaration to make. After learning that Signora Frola had nothing but kind words for Ponza, but that the community finds his treatment of her to be harsh and even cruel, he announces that Signora Frola is mad. He states that her madness dates back four years, to when her daughter died. As is explained, Signora Ponza is Ponza's second wife, and not Signora Frola's daughter. Ponza relates the details of her madness, and suggests that for her own well-being he keeps up appearances.

Having explained his situation to the sympathy of all involved, Ponza takes his leave, after which Dina and Agazzi suggest that they had their suspicions. As they discuss the Signora's madness, Signora Frola reappears. She notes the groups changed perception of her, and wishes to set them straight about her son-in-law. Signora Frola then explains that it is Ponza who is lying (although she takes care to defend him from being labeled mad) and that he has fabricated the story of her madness to conceal the truth of the situation. She then tells the story of how her daughter became terribly sick and was removed from Ponza's care. Ponza began to believe that she had died, and when presented with his much-recovered wife, refused to accept her. They then staged a second wedding in order to reunite the couple. She further explains that he keeps her locked away so as not to have his wife taken from him again. Signora Frola again takes her leave, and Laudisi steps forward saying laughingly, "So you're having a look at each other? Well! And the truth?" thus closing Act I.

Act II begins in Agazzi's study with Agazzi on the phone, and Laudisi and Sirelli waiting expectantly. Agazzi is searching for information regarding the neighboring town, but to his dismay, everything has been destroyed and all of the survivors relocated. At this point Laudisi offers the advice that they believe both stories or believe neither story. Laudisi suggests that the documentation they seek will provide little in terms of truth, for the truth is located in the mind and not in documents. Insisting on possessing facts, the men agree to bring Ponza and Frola in together, at which point the ladies enter the room. Agazzi instructs them to visit on Signora Frola, and conjure up an excuse for to bring her back with them. While they do that, Agazzi will go to his office, intentionally forgetting a brief that requires Ponza's attention, only so that he might bring Ponza back with him.

All leave with the exception of Laudisi who paces the room, and pauses in front of a mirror. Addressing the image in the mirror, Laudisi asks who is mad, and points a finger at the image. Indeed Laudisi and the image point at each other in accusation as Laudisi states that everyone carrys such a phantom within. At this point the Butler enters announcing the arrival of Signora Cini and another woman. Cini introduces her friend as Signora Nenni, a friend of hers who has come to meet Signora Agazzi. Laudisi explains the plan to Cini and Nenni, stating that the truth is already known and suggesting all that remains is the unmasking. When Cini asks who is mad, Laudisi tells her to guess. When she guesses that it is Ponza, Laudisi tells her she is correct, and then mentions the certificate of the second marriage. When Cini suggests the certificate would mean that she is mad, again Laudisi says that she is correct. As Cini questions the validity of the certificate, Laudisi states that it "has just the value that each of you chooses to give it."

As Laudisi creates doubt among the women, Dina enters explaining that they have looking at the letters written between the mother and the daughter. Having seen the letters and having heard Frola talk, the women are convinced that it is Ponza who is mad. Laudisi is convinced by their certainty that it must then be Frola who is mad.

As the women adjour to the drawing room, as instructed by Agazzi, Laudisi begins to challenge Dina's convictions. He suggests that if she is convinced that the matter is closed she should disobey Agazzi's instructions and shut the door between the two rooms. After they discuss the matter of the door, Frola begins to play the piano in the other room, and the two hurry in to hear her. The stage remains empty for a moment, after which, Ponza and Agazzi appear—Ponza catching the last few notes.

Agazzi continues with his planned charade of having forgotten important paperwork when he too hears the music. The two men approach the doorway at which time Ponza realizes that it is Frola who is playing. Ponza is visibly upset by the situation and claims that the song Frola is playing used to be played by his wife. As he grows more emotional, Ponza suggests that by their meddling, they are killing Frola. When the music ceases and the listeners applaud, Frola says, "But you should hear how my Lena plays." This upsets Ponza further. Sirelli then appears (watchful and concerned over Ponza's state) and is instructed to show the ladies in.

A tense and violent exchange takes place during which Frola shares "glances of understanding" with the other women. Ponza questions Frola about what she has been saying, and explains that of course Lena hasn't played as she has been dead for four years. When Ponza asks Frola to say the name of his second wife, she says with a wink "Her name is Julia!" Ponza accuses Frola of trying to ruin him, and breaks into sobs. As Frola tries to comfort Ponza, she asks that the ladies support her claim that she has always said that her daughter was dead. Ponza orders the Signora out of the room, and upon her leaving, admits that he had enacted the scene to keep up the illusion. Ponza leaves the rest of the party dumbfounded, and Laudisi steps forward and says laughingly, "And so, ladies and gentlemen, we learn the truth!"

Act III begins with Laudisi "sprawling in an easy chair, reading a book." The Butler enters with the police commissioner Centuri. The commissioner reveals that he has unearthed evidence from Ponza's town, and hands the communications over to Laudisi for him to look at. Laudisi, who at first makes sounds of intrigue and satisfaction, ends his perusal with a sigh of disappointment. Laudisi insists that the documents prove nothing, and suggests that the commissioner destroy them and invent a more clear, more concrete communication. Offended by Laudisi's suggestion, the commissioner asks that Laudisi fetch Agazzi. From the other room come cheers as Agazzi, Sirelli, Dina, Laudisi, Cini, Nenni, Amalia, Signora Sirelli, and several others enter the room. They are excited that they will at last learn the truth.

Centuri hands the documents over to Agazzi, at which point Laudisi informs the crowd that the papers reveal a former neighbor of Ponza testified that Signora Frola was in a sanatorium. Agazzi corrects Laudisi stating that the document only says the Frola woman, at which point it is assumed the neighbor was talking about the daughter. It is then revealed that the witness was not a neighbor of Ponza's, but only visited the town frequently. With doubt cast yet again over the situation, Laudisi suggests that the Prefect use his authority to order Ponza's wife to speak. While all agree this is the best idea Laudisi has had, it comes to light that nobody has actually seen the second wife. To this, Laudisi suggests that she is perhaps a phantom—for either Ponza or Frola.

The commissioner returns indicating that the prefect is approaching with Ponza. The prefect who sides with Ponza on the matter intends to visit with Signora Frola. Agazzi suggests to the prefect the possibility that it is Ponza and not Frola who is mad, at which point the prefect asks Laudisi's opinion. Laudisi again suggests that both Ponza and Frola can be believed. Frustrated with Laudisi, Agazzi and Sirelli reiterate Laudisi's earlier suggestiong that the prefect talk to the wife.

When Ponza is asked to enter the room so that the prefect can ask to speak to his wife, Ponza resigns before the question can be asked. The men discuss the options, and the Prefect states his belief in Ponza, but he too wants to satisfy his curiosity. Ponza refuses to acquiesce. When the prefect suggests that he might be able to question Ponza's wife without Ponza's consent, Ponza agrees to bring her to Agazzi's.

Ponza exits and the men discuss Ponza's refusal to hire a servant. Before Ponza can return with his wife, Signora Frola enters weeping. The Prefect wants her sent away, and she suggests that she will leave the town immediately. As Signora Frola pleads with the Prefect, a hush falls over the group and a lady appears dressed in "deep mourning." Frola and Signora Ponza embrace, and then Frola and Ponza leave the room. At this point, Signora Ponza states that she is the daughter of Frola, and the second wife of Ponza. She then states, "and, for myself, I am nobody!" Claiming that she is who they believe her to be. As usual, Laudisi has the final words, "And there, my friends, you have the truth! Are you satisfied?"

Right You Are
(If You Think You Are)

Lamberto Laudisi functions as the wisdom of the play, the one who understands, though he cannot know all. His amusement as well as his primary concern is that the others in the play are determined to discover the "truth" about Signor and Signora Ponza and Signora Frola, newcomers to their village.

Amalia is Laudisi's sister and wife to Agazzi, who is Signor Ponza's superior. She shares some of Laudisi's intelligence and some of her friends' insatiable curiosity.

Agazzi, husband to Amalia, has a somewhat exalted sense of his importance in the community and enjoys having the power to insure that Signor Ponza and Signora Frola are not again rude to his wife and daughter Dina.

Dina, the daughter of Amalia and Agazzi, becomes as involved in the quest as her mother and father, though she enjoys Laudisi's wit, despite her frustration at his teasing her about her curiosity.

Signor and Signora Sirelli have an ordinary, bickering marriage in which neither accepts the word of the other. They are both very interested in what others do and how they live, hence their involvement, in the Ponza and Frola affair.

Signora Cini is a malicious old woman who pretends to be innocent, amiable, and inexperienced.

Signor Ponza is new to town as a government employee with a strange living arrangement. He claims that his mother-in-law refuses to accept the death of her daughter, his first wife.

Signora Frola is Ponza's mother-in-law. She maintains that Ponza went mad when his wife was taken away from him, and that he believed his wife wife died in a sanatorium.

Prefect is the govorner of the town and Ponza's boss.

Centuri is the police commissioner.

CRITICAL VIEWS ON
Right You Are
(If You Think You Are)

MAURICE SLAWINSKI ON HUMANS' INSATIABLE CURIOSITY ABOUT OTHERS

[Maurice Slawinski is a Lecturer in Italian Studies and a member of the School of Modern Languages at Lancaster University (England). He has co-edited *Science, Culture and Popular Belief in Renaissance Europe* (Manchester, 1991). He is also co-editor of the comparative literature journal, *New Comparison*.]

Così è (se vi pare) is generally seen as the first landmark in Pirandello's experimentation with theatrical form, the beginning of his preoccupation with theatre within theatre, a powerful subversion of the conventions of bourgeois drama, and his first consciously 'philosophical' play. It is not a text closely associated with the present critical interest in the playwright's representation of gender roles and female sexuality. Two of the ingredients of this heady mixture are already in place: the conflicting, mutually exclusive passions of maternal and marital possession. Yet central though they are to the story told (or rather, the impossibility of telling *that* story) they are less than central to the author's construction, and the spectators' reception of the play. Maternal love is not so much explored in *Così è*, as simply given, the 'universally acknowledged truth' (except that the two sides cannot agree what forms it should 'naturally' take) upon which both the Agazzi family's objections to their neighbour's domestic arrangements and Mrs Frola's successive explanations of them are based. Sexual desire is only briefly hinted at as a possible reason for Mr Ponza's presumed incarceration of his wife. (...)

And quite unlike any other Pirandellian heroine, the childless (metaphorically virginal) Mrs Ponza appears quite unmarked either by sexual or by maternal feeling.

All this points us in the direction of asking questions about the all-too-realistic inquisitiveness of Counsellor Agazzi's family and friends—and confronting our own rather than investigating the sexual pathology of a 'sventura' which for all the emotional naturalism of its representation can scarcely be accounted for in terms of the social and psychological realism proper of 'drawing-room' theatre.[1] It is in the conflict between these two worlds (almost a play within a play) that the overt significance of the text lies, both as a fable concerning the impossibility of establishing objective truths in the realm of human behaviour, and as a discourse on the nature of artistic representation, foreshadowing the more explicit discussion of this theme to be found in *Sei personaggi in cerca d'autore*. *Così è* is a 'trial by curiosity'. In the dock stands a family whose existence in the eyes of their self-appointed, public-minded inquisitors appears perversely private. The latter, ranged around them in the drawing-room-turned-trial-chamber, are in turn gradually made to appear to us, the audience beyond the proscenium arch, obscenely curious. (...)

There is an excess (of emotions, of meanings, of silences) in the interlocking stories of Mr Ponza and Mrs Frola, and the fact that they cannot be sustained save through the sacrifice (murder or suicide?) of the third party to their mystery, which no reading of the play as a moral-aesthetic allegory can quite put to rest, and makes Mrs Ponza's brief appearance the most charged and unsettling female presence in Pirandello's theatre. (...)

She who throughout the play, by her very absence, had been the real focus of our gaze, turns that gaze back upon us at the last. The challenge to the audience seems to me more complex than simply daring us to acknowledge a social taboo. There is no denying the darkly sexual roots of the *sventura* which afflicts the Ponza-Frola family, and of the curiosity, voyeuristic compulsion, which it arouses among the *ben pensanti* around them (it is voiced at the outset, as we have seen, by none other than the supposedly detached Laudisi). But the suggestion of a profound sexual trauma, deeply embedded as it is in the play's structure, does not appear to me to be central to its meaning. (...)

For it is in the process of looking itself, rather than the whys and wherefores of Mr Ponza's unusual domestic arrangements, that the play's sexual charge ultimately lies. The theatrical gaze which Pirandello constructs, how we look at the inquisitors looking at the characters standing centre stage, is not neutral but gendered, and that gendering of the gaze is compounded not merely of sexual prurience, but of the whole complex of social relations rooted in sexual difference, from the forms of sexual gratification to those of filial piety. These operate at all levels of the play-text, encompassing not only the Frola-Ponza family, but also their inquisitors, the way that in pursuit of their curiosity they act out their own conflicts as spouses, parents, children. And they extend beyond the characters on stage, to us, the audience, men and women, watching in turn. The play is indeed 'about' sexual violence, but the implicit, unspecified violence committed on Mrs Ponza is not so much its meaning as its driving force, that which sets in motion certain compulsions among those looking on (the inquisitors within the proscenium arch, and the audience outside it). The real subject is the violence of the gaze, that way of looking, understanding, appropriating *sexually* which the unspoken, unspeakable infraction makes manifest. What I want to argue is that over and above its 'philosophical' and 'theatrical' novelty, this play-text establishes a new problematic of gender. In this reading, *Così è* is a text about how 'we' (men, a theatre audience, male-dominated society) look at women, and how women look back. (...)

That curiosity—the compulsion to look at the unusual, exceptional, hidden, and make sense of it—may be more than simply a dramatic pretext for Pirandello is clearly signalled at the outset of *Così è*, in an exchange which has received surprisingly little attention. The question it poses is precisely what this curiosity is which will drive the plot forward and keep the audience hooked, keep us looking at Laudisi looking at the inquisitors looking at their quarry, who, in the final moment of the play, in the person of Mr Ponza, turn the gaze back whence it came. (...)

Curiosity, the act of looking at and questioning what is

unusual, is 'natural', something we cannot attribute merely to others. That much is uncontroversial, the whole effectiveness of the play, its hold on the audience, depends upon it. But the exchange also highlights, from the outset, the fact that for all his intellectual superiority Laudisi himself cannot claim to be without this fundamental human trait, cannot exclude himself from humanity. (...)

Laudisi suffers from the stigma attaching to all of those (male) *dramatis personae* of Pirandello's plays (...)

an excessive trust in their own, superior *male* intelligence, which falters here, for an instant, as Laudisi is caught out unexpectedly by the no less rigorous logic of his 'clever little' niece, and which will falter again with much more tragic consequences, in later plays. (...)

Dina searches an instant for a suitable absurdity, 'che so', then mentally places the cook's shoes on a drawing-room side-table. The object, from Dina's point of view, may be chosen at random. But within the context of the play it underscores—indeed prefigures—the whole essence of the situation. Something which should not be there, something belonging to a lower level of society, is to be placed under scrutiny because it offends the sense of order of this bourgeois household. And that something, the shoes of a female underling (for that seems to me the essential point behind their comic specificity), points to three further elements which are not unique to *Così è*, but are characteristic of Pirandello's plays in general. In the first place, the relationships he portrays, social or personal, are always, quite explicitly power relations, based on the dominance of class, or sex, or, as in the case of this 'founding' text, both together. Second, the 'problem' which sets the play in motion invariably involves a challenge to the dominance of bourgeois patriarchy (be it only so slight as the desire of the underlings to keep their private lives private). Third, the battle that ensues is not a struggle for control of the means of production (or reproduction) but for control of meaning: whose point of view shall determine the truth. (...)

By the end, uncle and niece have reached a tacit agreement, if not about what they are likely to discover, at least about the necessity of allowing the confrontation to go ahead. One may seek proof of male subjection of women, the other confirmation of the relativity of truth, but both *need* it to take place in order to confirm their own truth to themselves, as indeed does the third player in this exchange, the absent father, who has invested in the credibility of Mr Ponza. It is an accord which will continue into Act III, when Laudisi will propose, Dina second and Agazzi execute the interrogation of Mrs Ponza. (...)

Mrs Ponza is quite simply and unmistakably a woman, hence from the view of a phallocentric gaze, 'nessuna, nessuna'. But in her refusal to represent herself she is also, in Lacan's psychoanalytical foregrounding of Saussurian linguistics, the equal and opposite term, the feminine 'zero', without which the masculine 'one' is also nothing. She is that which makes possible the play of difference. (...)

As Pirandello's stage directions stand, Mrs Ponza enters alone and unannounced, (...)

a woman looking unflinchingly into the blinding centre, not concealing from herself what is not there but seeing as in a mirror her sister, her similar, *nessuna*: the truth of a state which is also her own.

This contrasts sharply with another, more literal look in the mirror, which occurs almost in the exact middle of the play. There (II.4) it is Laudisi who looks, and ironically fails to recognise himself in a mirror, in an unwitting parody of the mirror-stage, that moment when the child first recognises itself in the image reflected by a mirror, which Lacan takes as the threshold of separation of self from other, the primal moment of the subject's entry into the symbolic, the world of meaning and representation.[18] It is the defining moment of his vanity, his love of himself as possessor of a superior truth (narcissism, according to Freud, is precisely the inability fully to recognise oneself as self, in Lacanian terms an incomplete mirror stage, where the self retains a degree of otherness and remains an object of desire). But there is a third player in the drama, looking now with Dina, now with Laudisi, whose gaze is directed as into a mirror: the audience. What of that to us, what do we see? (...)

At the last, we see not ourselves, but a woman looking back. And that gaze has been positioned in such a way that we cannot evade it, search its periphery for some signifier that will cover its nakedness. Laudisi's final self-confirming laugh rings hollow. Our own fetishism has been called. We are confronted instead with the impossibility of continuing to look in that fashion. The compelling need is not just for *pietà*, but for other ways of producing meaning.

That might sound like an ending. It is the ending of the play, but it is the beginning of Pirandello's theatre, the premise of a struggle for control of meaning which will repeatedly challenge the male discourses of power and penetration and point to ways in which women can construct their own truth, impress it even upon men and not simply acquiesce in their own denial. (...)

Pirandello the quasi-marxist about to turn fascist-fellow-traveller of 1917 might have found it difficult to see himself as post-modern feminist *avant la lettre*. But that is not the point at issue. The point is that his play-text is genuinely, originally productive—not merely reproductive—of meaning for us, that it turns round our curiosity.

Notes

1. This counterpointing of psychological naturalism (attaching to characters who are emotionally credible, but whose *dramma* is consciously forced beyond the bounds of social and psychological verisimilitude) and satirical stereotyping (of characters whose social and psychological motivations, for all the one-dimensional parody of their portrayal, are eminently credible) is wonderfully brought out in the 1972 Giorgio De Lullo production (originally for the Compagnia dei Giovani, and later broadcast by RAI in a filmed reconstruction of the original stage version subsequently made commercially available on video-tape), though I am unconvinced by the ever-sympathetic, emotionally attractive Laudisi of this production.

18. Jacques Lacan, 'Le stade du miroir comme formateur de la fonction du Je', *Ecrits*, cit., pp. 93–100.

—Maurice Slawinski, "Le Scarpe Della Serva: Another Look at
Così è (Se Vi Pare)," *The Yearbook of the Society for Pirandello Studies*
14 (1994): pp. 26–27, 29, 31–32, 46, 49, 50–51.

ANN HALLAMORE CAESAR ON THE SOCIAL IMPULSE

[Ann Hallamore Caesar's *Characters and Authors in Luigi
Pirandello* was published by the Clarendon Press, Oxford,
in 1998.]

Così è (se vi pare) marks an important moment in Pirandello's
literary career, for it prefigures the concerns that will dominate
his theatre in the 1920s. (...)

By the beginning of the play every tragedy that could possibly
happen to a family appears to have happened to them—death,
insanity, illness, and the loss of all they possessed. The three
(daughter, mother, and son-in-law) arrive to make a new start in
an unfamiliar provincial town after an earthquake devastated
their home town. All their possessions have been lost in the
ruins, so there is no way of confirming who they are, or clarifying
what exactly the circumstances are which led to such an
unconventional, and in the eyes of the community, unnatural
lifestyle. The domestic arrangements whereby the mother-in-
law is lodged in an apartment in an affluent part of town while
her daughter lives in much reduced circumstances on the
outskirts become a source of endless aggravation for the
townspeople. Combine the oddity of their living arrangements
with the husband's practice of spending stretches of time each
day with his mother-in-law, while she in her turn is only allowed
to see her daughter from a distance by standing in the courtyard
below her apartment, and one can begin to understand why they
are the target of such gossip. At the outset of the play, the
audience is encouraged to feel similarly intrigued by the
irregularity of their domestic arrangements and concur with the
townspeople's curiosity to know more.

Even allowing for the difference in social codes between
eighteenth-century provincial life in England as articulated by

Jane Austen and early twentieth-century small town communities in Sicily as represented by Luigi Pirandello, the patterns of behaviour depicted are remarkably similar. Newcomers arrive in the district, and social calls are paid both to extend a welcome and also, less charitably but more imperatively, to satisfy what one of the characters, a young woman called Dina, describes as 'la curiosità naturalissima di tutto il paese' ('the very natural curiosity of the community'). (Dina at 19 is old enough to be part of an adult world, but young enough not to identify fully as yet with its practices; she still has insight—an attribute that is palpably absent from her mother. A few lines earlier Dina had referred to her mother's circle as being 'cortesi per curiosità' ('courteous out of curiosity'), a curiosity that soon turns to suspicion). Respectable members of the small town community assiduously visit each other at home, urged on by their thirst for enlightenment, while snobbery provides a further stimulus to their curiosity, for Signora Frola has taken an apartment next door to her son-in-law's superior, the consigliere Agazzi. But what begins as a slightly uneasy, but none the less not unreasonable attempt at sociability soon degenerates, as it becomes increasingly evident that the newcomers do not wish to comply with the unwritten social code. By refusing to engage with the normal exchange of courtesies, the family cannot be assimilated into the community and the townspeople adopt a correspondingly hostile and inquisitorial role. Worse still, mother and son-in-law not only refuse to explain their behaviour, but each offers, on separate occasions, different versions of the family's recent past that would, if they were true, cancel each other out. While we learn from Signor Ponza that his mother-in-law is mad and does not realize that her daughter is dead and he is now living with his second wife, Signora Frola tells us that it is her son-in-law who is mad and she and her daughter have agreed between them on the fiction that she is his second wife, so as not to upset his belief that he was previously married to a woman now dead. Drawing-room chat in Act I soon gives way to a more inquisitorial approach—adding a new sinister dimension to that word 'confession' that we will later see used to describe the purpose of the salon in *Vestire gli ignudi*. What has the makings of being a metaphysical thriller slowly transforms before the audience's eyes into a disconcerting exercise in psychological torture. (...)

At the end of the play Ponza tells Agazzi that he wishes to resign from his post, 'perchè non posso tollerare quest'inquisizione accanita, feroce sulla mia vita privata'[28] ('because I cannot tolerate this heartless, ferocious inquisition into my private life'). Using the gossip generated by the arrival of the family and the successive interviews which an inner circle of townspeople conduct with each member of the family one by one, the play traces the decline in their attitude from curiosity to obsession, from the importunate to the persecutory. The small circle of inquisitors widens as others visit them, urged on by a need to know more. (...)

Behind the enigma presented by the newcomers lies another, namely why this irregular but somewhat featureless family grouping should arouse such extremes of curiosity. It is a question that is foregrounded at the outset of the story by the narrator, but it is not directly posed in the play. 'La signora Frola e il signor Ponza, suo genero' has in common with very many of Pirandello's tales all the hallmarks of orality. The narrator speaks to his interlocutors directly over the heads of the community to which he belongs, while at the same time using the full range of ironic devices, from antiphrasis to mockery, to ensure that we understand that he is not party to the distress exhibited by his fellow citizens. In inviting us to resolve the central enigma— what precisely is the relationship between Signora Frola and Signor Ponza? is he or is he not her son-in-law?—he also makes it clear that what perturbs him is not the problem itself, but the effect it is having on the community; 'ma dico di tenere cosi sotto quest'incubo, un'intera cittadinanza vi par poco?'[30] 'but I ask you, to keep a whole town on tenterhooks, doesn't that seem serious enough to you?'). The reader is made to feel that the degree of consternation these 'forestieri eccentrici' ('eccentric strangers') bring to the community is out of all proportion to the cause. If gossip were concerned only with social control, a glue that holds the community together, the reaction here would have to be read as excessive. The storyteller hints at another reason. (...)

Incest provides a solution to the conundrum presented, but in so doing it goes against the current of a play whose internal logic would seem to demand a lack of resolution, an open-endedness that is irritating both to the inner circle on stage and the outer circle constituted by the audience. (...)

It is true that story and play were written in 1917, at a time when Pirandello's home life was still torn apart by his wife's accusations of incest, but even in *Sei personaggi in cerca d'autore*, incest is arguably the most important, but not the only aspect of an encounter that reeks of squalor and compromise—both sexual and economic. Disgust for the body and its proclivities that is so compellingly communicated in *Sei personaggi* is quite absent in *Così è (se vi pare)* which must count as being amongst the least physical, or the most metaphysical, of Pirandello's plays. The possibility of incest is referred to and there is nothing in the play that rules it out, but it is present in a curiously abstract way as no more than a potential explanation for the newcomers' unconventional behaviour. (...)

To return to the original question: why does the failure to tease out the mystery surrounding the newcomers bring such perturbation in its wake? Whereas in the other narratives of identity referred to in this chapter, the protagonists are, for better or for worse, affected by the gossip that circulates about them, in *Così è (se vi pare)* they appear to be immune to public opinion. Bound up in the network of identities they have created for each other, they do not require further validation and refuse to enter the normal processes of social interaction by which each of us comes to know ourselves. But, by the same token, it suggests that there is nothing noble about being an outsider, nothing heroic.

Pirandello's theatre, like much of his narrative, is concerned with the individual as a social being. Whatever the lengths his characters go to to try to divest themselves of the imprint other people, families, and whole communities have left on them (and some, like Mattia Pascal in *Il fu Mattia Pascal* and Vitangelo Moscarda in *Uno, nessuno e centomila*, as we shall see in the next chapter, will go to extraordinary lengths to do so), his characters remain saturated in the social. Pirandello's work, both drama and narrative, is taken up with questions of how we talk with each other, why we talk about each other, what we do to each other when we talk in these ways, and what we do to ourselves.

NOTES

26. Luigi Pirandello, *Così è (se vi pare)*, in *Maschere nude*, i (Milan, Mondadori, 1986), 438.

28. *Maschere nude*, i. 500.

30. 'La signora Frola e il signor Ponza, suo genero', in *Novelle per un anno*, iii/1. 777.

—Ann Hallamore Caesar, *Characters and Authors in Luigi Pirandello*, (Oxford: Clarendon Press, 1998): pp. 78–84.

DIANA A. KUPREL ON TRUTH'S ELUSIVE NATURE

[Diana Kuprel has taught at the University of Toronto. She has translated *Medallions* (Jewish Lives) by Zofia Nakowska (Northwestern University Press, 2000).]

Throughout his literary *oeuvre*, Pirandello engages, discursively and demonstratively, in an explicit ontological enquiry into the very nature of identity, conceiving of it as a particular manifestation of an underlying process of cognition, the object of which evades any categorical determination. He interposes and dialectically engages two paradigms: that of *idem*-identity (or sameness) and that of *ipse*-identity (or selfhood as, in part, a function of the other).[1] (...)

Pirandello sets up a traditional, Aristotelian dramatic pattern in *Così è*: there is a movement towards knowledge through interviews with witnesses and the search for and through documents. More precisely, the author stages a basic hermeneutic situation, the object of which is to know an unknown. This situation is initiated *vis-à-vis* the introduction of an alterity—namely, the Ponza family, who are described as 'strangers' ('forestieri')—into a familiar realm. (...)

It is not, however, the final establishing of an indisputable truth that is at issue here; rather, as each explanation serves only to open up more questions, as the identity of Signora Ponza is never determined unequivocally and absolutely—in short, as final knowledge is constantly displaced—what is at issue is *the process of truth-finding*. 'Truth' does not take a propositional character, but rather, an interrogative character. (...)

In each of the three acts, Pirandello highlights a certain paradigm of truth-finding. Each paradigm hinges on the notion of truth as final and apodictic. Each is undermined or shown to be inadequate through a dialectical encounter with a paradigm of truth as a mode of participatory disclosure. This self-reflexive paradigm takes into account the diversity of the 'interpreting mood' which, as it were, giving 'to the same sound a different intensity of meaning',[12] imprints on the thing to be known a particular, never reiterable form. This dialectic of paradigms structures the attempt to establish an unknown person's identity. Pirandello gives voice to the paradox that *idem*-identity, while existing, is unknowable; while each individual appearance of the person does represent the person, because it is a particular originating in the knower's or observer's situatedness (*ipse*-identity), the appearance can never truly coincide with the person; only the for- and through-others are truly knowable.

At the end of Act I, the empirical model of truth based on naive realism is debunked. This model is grounded in the belief that perception (here, vision and touch) grants the first and truest access to reality. (...)

Laudisi offers a critique of the empirical model. Early on, he attempts to dissuade the others from thinking that things are as we see them by 'saying and showing' that bare sensation (touch and sight) preceding all formation is but an empty abstraction, that the given must always be taken in a definite aspect, from the individual viewpoint of the observer, and so apprehended as something that is subject to change. (...)

After the empirical model is shown to be inadequate, the verificative model is tried and tested. The questions which seek an unqualifiable answer are: Which one—Signor Ponza or Signora Frola—is telling the truth? Which one is mad? Thus a search is instituted for documents—e.g. birth, marriage and death certificates—, and witnesses who can confirm whose truth-claim carries a truth-value. The witness, however, was but an occasional visitor to the town and did not know the family personally, while the document of a second marriage may be inauthentic (it may have been concocted to preserve Ponza's delusion that he is marrying another woman). As Laudisi states, documents, like the letters Signora Ponza writes to Signora Frola, have no independent truth-value, only 'il valore che ognuno gli vuol dare' (p. 1069) ['the value that each person gives to them'].

Finally, in the third act, the quest for truth becomes an explicit ontological inquest. The testimonial paradigm of truth-finding as truth-saying (*parlare*) or assertion, which is based on the questioning of the object by a tribunal authority and which requires that the object respond apophantically,[14] comes under fire from the very object of the inquest. Signora Ponza, believed to be the only person who can confirm either Signor Ponza's or Signora Frola's stories by testifying as to who she is, or rather, the relational interconnection (no relation/second wife or daughter/ first wife) which she bears with each of the scrutinized characters, refuses to subject herself to this process. The veiled subject, who would be unveiled, will not be unveiled. (...)

Signora Ponza thus stands as the corporeal site of a chiasm, or intertwining, of the passive and the active. This locus is figured in the veil that she wears and the dual function that it fulfils. On the one hand, the visual image of identity rendered a *tabula rasa*, it is a self-reflexive blank screen onto which, as Bonnie Marranca aptly notes, 'the community projects its own scenario'.[16] Acknowledging that she is both Signora Frola's daughter and Signor Ponza's second wife—that is, that she has no independent existence but is the one whom others take her to be—she declares herself to be a hybrid composed of elements from diverse origins, constituted by other people. She exists purely within a triadic situation of relationality to others. On the other hand, the veil functions to recall 'the closure of private space [...], the injunction of no trespassing upon this space'.[17] By actively refusing to declare herself to be 'either/or' and, moreover, by attending with concern to the suffering of others (Signor Ponza and Signora Frola) against the invasiveness of third parties, she speaks on behalf of an ethics of empathy that calls for an interpretation that obeys, or listens to, the injunction starting from the other. (As Ricoeur points out in 'On Accusation', the Latin *obedientia*, meaning *obedience*, is related to *obaudire*, which means *to give ear to, to listen*.)[18] In doing so, she subverts the process of truth-finding under the umbrella of objectivism—that is, as the locating of a single, determinable, unchangeable meaning—in favour of truth as, at least in part, an autobiographical affair, a function of subjectivity, as subjectivity that is in itself unfixable in any final form. She leaves the others with themselves.

Notes

1. See Paul Ricoeur's excellent study of the philosophical ground for the paradigms of *idem*-identity and *ipse*-identity in *Oneself as Author*.

12. This is Wilhelm von Humboldt's phrase: 'The difference in the interpreting mood gives to the same sound a different intensity of meaning; in all expression, something not absolutely determined by the words seems as if it were to overflow from there' (cited in Ernst Cassirer, *The Philosophy of Symbolic Forms*, pp. 50–51).

14. Heidigger addresses the apophantic nature of assertion in *The Basic Problems of Phenomenology*: 'The primary character of assertion is apophansis [...]. Translated literally, it means the exhibiting of something from its own self, *apo*,
    letting it be seen as it is in itself, *phainesthai*. The basic structure of assertion is the exhibition of that about which it asserts' (p. 209).

16. Bonnie Marranca, 'Pirandello: A Work in Progress', p. 159.

17. Malek Alloula, *The Colonial Harem*, p. 13.

18. Paul Ricoeur, 'On Accusation', pp. 72–73.

—Diana A. Kuprel, "The Hermeneutic Paradox: Pirandello's Così è (Se Vi Pare)," *Journal of the Society for Pirandello Studies*, 17 (1997): pp. 46–56.

[Jerome Mazzaro was a Professor of Modern
Languages and Literatures for over 30 years at the
University of Buffalo. In his prolific career, he has
published numerous essays on Pirandello's work. He is
also the author of *Transformations in the Renaissance
English Lyric* (Cornell University Press, 1970) and
William Carlos Williams: The Later Poems (Cornell
University Press, 1973).]

The questioning of the basis of these mathematical axioms by
David Hilbert in the late nineteenth century led to their being
seen as self-evident assumptions "about space (or objects in
space)" and a consequent increased reliance by mathematicians
on assumed models. Within these models, they concentrated on
consistency and the principle "that logically incompatible
statements cannot be simultaneously true," though, as Bertrand
Russell later argued, even within the framework of elementary
logic, contradiction may be constructed "that is precisely
analogous to the contradiction first developed in the Cantorian
theory of infinite classes."[1] It is to this principle of resolving
incompatible statements that Luigi Pirandello addresses both his
play *Così è (se vi pare)* (*Right You Are [If You Think So]*, 1917) and
his earlier tale "La signora Frola e il signor Ponza, suo genero"
(1915) on which the play is based.

In both, people are asked to arrive at truth by choosing
between incompatible statements by Mrs. Frola and her son-in-
law. (...)

Even in cases where a narrator is intended to be uncredible, he
must be seen as "credibly uncredible." The point-of-view that
the Pirandello story establishes is that of a limited, anonymous
male who either is an inhabitant of Valdana and, therefore,
involved in the town's anguish or, much less likely, has heard of
the situation from someone who lives there and strongly
identifies with the town's dilemma. By failing to use first-person-
plural verbs, adjectives, and pronouns, he separates himself from
the townspeople, principally ladies, who are inclined to believe

Frola based on her good manners and a dislike of the son-in-law's appearance and conduct. The narrator divorces himself as well from the town's prefect, who is quite satisfied with Ponza's statement, presumably because, as Frola says, Ponza "is an excellent, a really excellent, secretary." Nor is he individually involved with the interests of Frola or Ponza, as he makes clear at the tale's onset, since "one, at least, has had the good luck to go mad, and the other to help him (or her) live out that madness." Thus he personally has no vested stake in the resolution of the pair's incompatible identifications of Mrs. Ponza except as their statements have led to an inability to tell fantasy from reality that threatens the town's sanity and spiritual health. Early, the narrator's advice for resolving the situation is for the prefect to order both principals out of town, and, later, he cites as the only certitude arising from the events, "a wonderful and most touching spirit of sacrifice which each has shown the other." (...)

The opening paragraphs, for example, identify Valdana as *una città disgraziata* (a dishonored city) ... *sotto quest'incubo* (under this nightmare/incubus) and needing to resolve the matter of Frola and Ponza *per la salute dell'anima degli abitanti* (for the health of the soul[s] of the inhabitants). Later, in her initial interview with the ladies of Valdana, Frola identifies her son-in-law's behavior with not cruelty but charity (*carità*), and in his rebutting remarks, the son-in-law states that it is out of charity that his second wife goes along with the charade and that such charity extends only so far. Indeed, one may argue that the story is not about Frola and the Ponzas at all but about the charitable way in which they live with their opposing certainties in contrast to the people of Valdana who, for their mental well-being, must seek intellectually to remove difference. (...)

Where there is no clearcut concept of evidence or, as in the case of Mrs. Ponza, of evidential support or when authorities (the ladies and the prefect) and testimony (Frola and Ponza) disagree and the evidence of things (Mrs. Ponza's notes) appears weak, decisions to accept are based, as Pirandello indicates, on benefit or self-interest. In terms of the ladies of Valdana, this interest centers on social acceptability; for the prefect, on work performance; for both Frola and Ponza, on preserving the appearances, if not the actuality, of sanity. However, for the narrator who registers no self-interest, nothing like a Pascal's wager emerges to direct his feelings toward either principal. (...)

Without advantage to be gained and equal or equally irrelevant benefits for either outcome, it is a matter of indifference which outcome he chooses. He manufactures "pseudo-benefits" to obscure and justify what critics often refer to as "idle curiosity," "nosiness," and intrusion. In doing so, the narrator allows Pirandello to display a condition which, in his essay *On Humor* (1908), he describes as "humoristic." Briefly, this condition is a "phenomenon of doubling in the act of conception." "From a mere realization of the contrary (*avvertimento del contrario*)," one arrives "at a sentiment, a feeling of the deeper issues involved (*sentimento del contrario*)," and "a conflict of emotions." For the humorist, this "*sentimento del contrario*" is part of a constitutive kindness, goodness, and "humaneness." (...)

Pirandello indicates that the origin of *Così è (se vi pare)*, and presumably the story on which it is based, is a terrifying dream in which he "saw a deep courtyard with no exit." Gaspare Giudice links this dream to the playwright's expressed feeling of having to combat the depths of a well (*pozzo*) from which he could not escape. Life had become distant, "devoid of meaning," and seemingly "more and more like a comic and crazy phantasmagoria."[6] The courtyard appears in the tale adjacent to and below the Ponzas' living quarters. It is the place from which Frola communicates with Mrs. Ponza orally and by notes. In the play, the courtyard is darkly shaded (*così buio*) and, according to Agazzi's daughter, looks like the well from which Pirandello in life sought to escape. Certainly, the claustrophobic sense of the dream explains the urgency and terror on which the narrator begins his tale. (...)

Little is said within the story about the exact nature of Ponza's and Frola's madness or even about the madness threatening the town, except that it involves a limited inability to distinguish fantasy from reality. As in other Pirandello works, the term provides a way of not dealing with certain situations. In what Giovanni Bussino calls "madness as a social fiction," it is a label which others impose on behavior and thinking that are unconventional. Rhetorically, the label serves to convey the narrator's agitated and dualistic state and, within the narrative (since mad people do not think or behave accountably), to justify his not having to integrate certain otherwise "incredible" details and events. These details and events are accepted by readers because the principals are labeled "mad." The label also assists Frola and Ponza in discrediting each other's arguments by negative *ad hominem* appeals. But, it should also be pointed out that positively the label allows the town to accept within limits the pair's living differently from its other citizens. Medically, except for their disagreements about Mrs. Ponza's identity, both Frola and Ponza appear to function sanely enough, and there is little evidence that, should the town go mad, as the narrator claims, it would become wholly dysfunctional. If Frola is to be believed, there may be in Ponza's actions elements of that "acute jealousy" which in Pirandello's wife Antonietta's behavior was diagnosed as "paranoid schizophrenia." The story's "madness" thus comes to resemble most nearly what R. D. Laing much later calls "schizoid" behavior. It echoes that "special strategy" to which individuals resort in order to persevere in unlivable situations. Commonly, as in the Pirandello story, these strategies reflect inabilities to resolve conflicting demands between conformity and instinctive energies.[8] (...)

Credibility in such a model occurs not in terms of point-of-view but in the probability of the action. This probability embraces total action and, within that action, individual character and character interaction. When thought and inner conflicts are involved, they necessitate the creations of devices (soliloquies, confidants, dream sequences) and situations by which this thought and conflict may be conveyed objectively to an audience. In creating these devices and situations from what had been narrative, writers often alter imagery, the numbers and durations of scenes, and the numbers and natures of characters. Their concern is not so much with the former narrator's ability to convince a reader as with the present characters' abilities to convince one another at the same time that they are also convincing audiences. Thus the faceless "citizens of Valdana" become concretely the Sirellis, Mrs. Cini, Mrs. Nenni, Ponza's immediate superior Commendatore Agazzi, his wife and daughter, other friends, and Lamberto Laudisi. What had been the persona of the narrator is now divided among several characters but mainly, as critics have argued, submerged into the character of Laudisi, who, it seems, also takes on aspects of that countervoice, conveying in the story the narrator's limitations. Gone are the tale's mathematical language and exaggerated urgency, and more palpably there are its widespread reliance on opinion and concern with stifling and restrictive social conventions.

The first act of *Così è (se vi pare)* consumes the bulk of what is contained in the story. (...)

Having tried authority and argument (mother and husband) to resolve the incompatible identifications of Mrs. Ponza, the play moves in the second act to evidence of things and theatrical confrontation. (...)

Act III returns to authority (the prefect and Mrs. Ponza) and evidence of things (affidavits) to conclude the issue of Mrs. Ponza's identity. (...)

In place of official records, they are asked to rely on a sworn statement from a man who recalls hearing of a woman being put into a nursing home. Whether she is Frola or Mrs. Ponza is unclear and, therefore, as useless as a guest's attempt to resolve the matter by analogy. In objecting to the comparison, another guest suggests the better idea of having the prefect interview the wife. Given the anxiety which the prefect finds on his arrival at the Agazzi apartment, he agrees to help, despite his own conviction that Ponza is telling the truth. Ponza's response to the interview is to request a transfer. Eventually, however, he agrees, provided that his mother-in-law is kept from seeing Mrs. Ponza. He will himself keep her away during the interview. While he is away getting his wife, more of the story's exposition is turned into Sirellian revelations. Frola arrives unexpectedly and offers to restore harmony by leaving town. Ponza enters with a woman whose face is heavily veiled. Frola embraces her immediately as her daughter Lina while Ponza keeps calling her Giulia. The woman asks the two to leave. They do so together, "exchanging affectionate caresses and whispered endearments." Approached, she admits to being both "the daughter of Signora Frola" and "the second wife of Signor Ponza." For herself, however, she is "neither one or the other"; she is "what others believe [her] to be." (...)

Indeed, the transformation of the Ponza–Frola situation from a narrative to a dramatic model allows what critics often cite as the major differences in Pirandello's handling of the two forms. It increases debate and dialectical play by making more explicit and active what had been implicit and reflective. Thus, for example, the townspeople's cruelty which in the story had been submerged in impersonal "scientific" language and the "urgency" of need is clearly brought into the open by Laudisi, Ponza, and Frola. At the start of the play, Laudisi exposes his sister's and niece's interests as potentially hurtful, and later, Ponza and Frola refer to the group's actions as a damaging "heartless, ferocious inquisition into [Ponza's] private life" and, despite their helpful intentions, doing "considerable harm." So, too, the philosophical debate about one's ability to know truth objectively, which in the story is "lost" in the narrator's privileged point-of-view and Pirandello's attack on *verismo*, is in the play emphasized both by the characters' independence of one another and the author and by a series of statements which Laudisi makes. At one point, he says that one "should show some respect for what other people see with their eyes and feel with their fingers, though it is the exact opposite of what you see and feel." At another, disclaiming the "truth" of documents, he indicates that for him "reality is to be found not in pieces of paper, but in the minds of ... people" and that no one has access to these minds apart from the little that people choose to reveal. The result is a work which, more than the story, appears to be formally in harmony with its emotional content and a thematic concern for "the slippery nature of truth: its relativity, its dependence on perspective, its detachment from mere fact, and its final, impossible ambiguity."[12] (...)

Pirandello calls the play a parable and adds in a letter to his son Stefano that it is "a great piece of devilry." In parable, as in other figural forms, there is the juxtaposition of a "known" vivid historical situation and an "un-" or "lesser known" abstract or intuited higher order. One has the sense of two situations competing for the same language and producing mystery. The purpose of the juxtaposition and competition is understanding through *ratio* or relations between. As Christ says in *Matthew* (13.11–17), parables are to be understood by the few and remain enigmatic to the uninitiated. Like the Parable of the Good Samaritan (*Luke* 10.30–37), they may be entirely worldly, the specific used to illustrate a type or principle, or, like the parables of the kingdom of heaven (*Matthew* 13.24–50), they may be used to reveal aspects of an afterlife. In either case, their mysteries are clarified through *interpretatio* rather than *expositio*, and, as distinct from other figural forms, parables rely on story or narrative models.[16] Pirandello's calling *Così è (se vi pare)* a piece of "devilry" suggests that, as opposed to the parables of Christ which assure the initiated with their telling, *Così è (se vi pare)* is intended to confuse or disrupt audiences with its unfolding. It likewise appears that its message is intended to be worldly rather than otherworldly. Mrs. Ponza does in fact appear on stage. What is in question for the group is her human, not her metaphysical identity, and one has in their failure to come to agreement something like William James' turning away in Pragmatism from verbal solutions, bad *a priori* reasons, fixed principles, closed systems, and pretended absolutes and origins. "Theories become instruments, not answers to enigmas, in which [one] can rest." One uses them not to lie back but to move forward in lockstep with and reaction to life's own dynamic thrusts.[17] (...)

For audiences what has made and continues to make the play immediately satisfying are not these mathematical and philosophical issues but the detective story nature of its action. *Così è (se vi pare)* misleads one into thinking that a mystery exists and will be solved. The solution, however, is deflected by issues of one's fitting into a community, the conditions of one's keeping a job, and a contest concerning the probability of objective truth. This last ends in the combined laughters of victory and released surplus psychic energy. Lost in these deflections by the play's having altered its premises are the epistemological and psychological discomforts of its not having finally solved the mystery.

NOTES

1. Bernard Knox, "Sophocles' Oedipus," in *Tragic Themes in Western Literature*, ed. Cleanth Brooks (New Haven: Yale Univ. Press, 1955), pp. 14, 18, 24; Ernest Nagel and James R. Newman, *Gödel's Proof* (New York: New York Univ. Press, 1958), pp. 14–15, 24.

6. Luigi Pirandello, as quoted in Gaspare Giudice's *Pirandello*, trans. Alastair Hamilton (London: Oxford Univ. Press, 1975), p. 179. A similar account was told to Raymond Cogniat in an interview for *Comoedia*, published in 1924; see ibid., p. 110.

8. Ibid., pp. [viii–ix]; Kenneth M. Hodess, "In Search of the Divided Self: A Psychoanalytic Inquiry into the Drama of Pirandello," in *Pirandello in America*, ed. Mario B. Mignone (Rome: Bulzoni, 1988), p. 136n.

12. Morris Freedman, "Moral Perspective in Pirandello," *Modern Drama*, 6 (1964), 369.

16. Giudice, *Pirandello*, p. 110. For a fuller discussion of parable, see my *The Figure of Dante: Essays on "The Vita Nuova"* (Princeton: Princeton Univ, Press, 1981), pp. 110–11.

17. William James, *Pragmatism* (New York: Washington Square Press, 1963), pp. 25–26. In noting a similarity between what James and Pirandello are turning *from*, I do not mean to suggest that they are necessarily always in agreement about what they are turning *toward*.

—Jerome Mazzaro, "Mathematical Certainty and Pirandello's Così è (Se Vi Pare)," *Comparative Drama* 28, 4 (1994–95): 439–56.

PLOT SUMMARY OF
Six Characters in Search of an Author

Set during the daytime in a theatre, *Six Characters*, traditionally, is without acts or scenes. The play is interrupted twice—once when the Father and the Stage Manager remove to "arrange the scenario," and a second time when the stage hands accidentally lower the curtain. The play opens on an empty stage; a rehearsal of Pirandello's play, *Mixing It Up*, is about to begin. The Prompter's box and a table and chair for the Manager occupy the stage. At this point, the actors and actresses wait for the Manager to arrive, who begins the dialogue of the play with a request to the Property Man to bring the lights up a bit. Three actors are on stage to begin the rehearsal. The Prompter begins to read the description of the setting for the act as the Manager determines the entrances and exits for the players. The Leading Man interrupts the Manager to ask if he "absolutely" must wear a cook's cap. Since the cap is written into the script, the Manager insists that he must. That it seems ridiculous has entirely to do, he says, with their not getting good French comedies and having to produce Pirandello's plays, in which Pirandello obscures all meaning and makes fools of the actors and audiences.

At this point and simultaneous with the Door-keeper's attempt to announce them, the Six Characters enter and come forward. As the Manager demands to know who they are, the Father explains that they are looking for an author, any author. Even the Manager would do since they must have an author, for they bring their drama with them. Perceiving them as mad, the Manager would have them leave immediately; the Father responds that their goals are virtually identical—to bring "life to fantastic characters on the stage," and their birth as characters is no more incomprehensible than many other life forms, trees, stones, water, or "woman." Hurt at their laughing at his explanation, he points to the mourning garb of the Mother. The Stepdaughter breaks in to plead for their existence, which has been "side-tracked." Regaining spirit from her description, the Father argues that a work of art, a character, cannot die; the actors and the Manager can impart life to them, eternal life. The Stepdaughter takes a different tack to reenter the argument, singing and dancing, gaining applause from the actors but annoyance from the Manager who thinks she is insane. She then describes scenes—sorrowful, outrageous, lascivious, contemptible— that will occur; caught in pain at what the Daughter previews, the Mother faints.

Intrigued that the woman in widow's garb is the Father's wife, the Manager himself becomes interested. The Father explains that the Mother "isn't a woman, she is a mother," that her drama exists only in the four children that she "had by two men." The Mother responds indignantly, accusing the Father of having "given" her to another man. Irritated that the Mother blames her life with that man (who was the Daughter's father), the Daughter argues that the Mother was happy with him, and that she denies that happiness only because of the Son who as a baby was sent away from her by the Father. The Mother again protests that she did not abandon her oldest child because of any fault or infidelity. The Father confesses that indeed it was his "doing."

The Father would defend himself, but his account incites the Daughter to present the disgraceful role he has played in her story. He begs to be allowed to speak before the Manager judges him unfairly. Each person's perception of events, despite the use of words common to all, makes understanding impossible, though each believes that he/she understands. The Father explains that he married the Mother because she was simple and humble, though she believed she was beneath him because of these qualities. The Father admits to being bored with her lack of "brain," and helping her relationship with his secretary so as to be free of her. He also admits to send the son away to a wet nurse in the country. However, as evidence that his motivation had been "pure," he presents that he had benevolently watched over the Stepdaughter as she grew up.

The Stepdaughter laughs at his rationalization of his actions, which she remembered and her mother had perceived as so dangerous that the little family moved away to deny him access to the young girl. The Father also maintains that the family lived in poverty since the death of the secretary because the Mother was too stupid to have gotten in touch with him for his support. When she wonders how she could possibly have known of his altruistic feelings, he responds that her fault lay in her never being able to guess his "sentiments." Nothing in their history has been his fault, he insists. He could hardly help his "miserable flesh" that forced him to go to Madame Pace where he once again met the Stepdaughter. Madame Pace had succeeded in employing the Stepdaughter in her brothel through the ploy of having the Mother mend her garments; when the Stepdaughter returns the mending, she declares that the Mother has failed to mend properly or has torn a garment. Rather than tell the Mother what has happened, the Stepdaughter absorbs the supposed damage or error through work as one of Madame Pace's "girls."

An "old client" of Madame Pace, the Father defends himself by accusing the Stepdaughter of "surprising" him in a place where she should not have known him; he protests that it was a mere moment that has caused her to ascribe to him a shameful character. This incident, however, permits the Stepdaughter to visit the Father and to "treat" the Father "in an equivocal and confidential manner," a manner that infuriates the Son, especially when he learns that her mother is his mother as well. Terming himself "an 'unrealized character,'" the Son separates himself from the entire situation. But his position destroys the Boy, who has lost his favored role as the only son of the little family and becomes a kind of charity case, dependent on the Father of the true Son.

Having grown interested, the Manager believes that the Characters are actually actors, failing to understand that they must have an author. The Father sees the Manager as their author; they need only someone to write out the scenes. Fully inclined by now, the Manager and the Six Characters go offstage to the Manager's office.

Act II begins with the Stepdaughter storming onstage from the office, declaring she will not be involved in what the Manager and the Father are creating. She brings the Child with her, and the Boy follows at some distance behind them. In the ensuing monologue, the Stepdaughter describes to the Child how her scene will happen and also explains the sorrow that the little girl experiences is because the Mother's attention has been entirely focused on the Son. Irritated with the Boy, the Stepdaughter yanks his hand from his pocket to discover the revolver with which he later will shoot himself. At this point, the Father and the Manager come to recover the Stepdaughter to finish the arrangements.

The Mother and the Son come onstage, though not together. She tries to talk with him, but he censures her for her life, accusing the Father as well. The Boy and the Child approach her, but she has no interest in anyone except the Son. Then the Actors, as well as the Manager, the Father, the Stepdaughter, the Prompter, the Property Man, and the Stage Manager, come onstage. Apart from the Actors, they all discuss the stage set that they will arrange; the Manager instructs the Prompter to reverse his role and take down in shorthand the dialogue of the Characters. The Actors are just to listen. The Father challenges the notion of a rehearsal, claiming that there is no necessity since the Characters are actually there. The Manager laughs at the thought that characters can act—only Actors can act. The Father cannot envision the Leading Lady as his wife. The Stepdaughter laughs at the actress chosen to play her role, whom she sees as inappropriate. The Manager will maintain that a character's shape is created by an actor, which causes the Father to understand finally why their author abandoned them.

For the Stepdaughter, the constructed scene bears no resemblance to the room she had described. The Manager is distressed that Madame Pace is not present; however, the father knows that she can be attracted by the "articles of her trade." She very soon appears and enters immediately into a soundless exchange with the Stepdaughter, and the play is underway. They whisper because the Father is outside the door in Madame Pace's brothel. The Manager insists the dialogue must be heard; she explains that it is the same litany of the Mother's work being badly done. The Manager who has stereotypical expectations of stock figures such as Madame Pace cannot accept her patois. The Mother responds in anger to Pace. The Stepdaughter sees her presence as an insult to the Mother; the Father sees her as a too-soon revelation of the "plot." Pace exits in anger at being insulted by the Mother.

The play begins once more with the encounter in Madame Pace's brothel between the Stepdaughter and the Father. The Mother, watching with the Son and the Child and the Boy, is in utter misery at the scene before her. When the Actors take their turn at performing the scene, the Father and the Stepdaughter see them as completely wrong. The Stepdaughter laughs uncontrollably; the Father tries to smooth things over, explaining their dismay at the transition from something that was once theirs and now belongs quite differently to the actors, an extension of the theme of *Right You Are* that encompasses the different perceptions which arise even from the repetition of another's words. The audience learns then the source of the Stepdaughter's anger at the beginning of Act II. The Father and the Manager have manipulated the scene in which the Stepdaughter and the Father meet at Madame Pace's. The scene now gives no cognizance of the Stepdaughter's pain at being required to disrobe for the Father who has perceived her mourning dress as mere trapping. The Stepdaughter would leave at this point, but the Manager convinces her to stay. She enters the scene with the Father, putting her head on his chest; the Mother discovers them and tries to separate them, screaming at the Father that he embraces her daughter.

Act III begins with additional scenery, trees, a fountain basin far in the side background. With the exception of the Boy and the Child, the Characters are all onstage, as well as the actors. The Stepdaughter tries to convince the Manager that the next scene should show them moving into the Father's house, despite the Son's objections. The Father enters into a discussion of the relative reality of the Manager and himself, declaring that a character has a solid, nonvarying existence, whereas a man—any human—lives a perpetually changing life, his reality constantly inconstant. The Manager accuses the Father of imitating an author whom he detests. The Father responds that he cannot imagine whom the Manager thinks of, but he himself knows that when a character is created, he becomes independent of the author. Then if the author should deny the character life, the character is nonetheless still alive and can only beg the author to give her/him a venue.

The Manager pulls the Father back into the planning of the action, which requires that the Boy be placed behind a tree rather than inside, so that the Child's scene, which must employ the fountain, can take place. The Son would go away, but he cannot since he is bound inextricably to the lives of the other Characters. He says that he has no role, and he has said nothing to the Mother, who has come to him so he may know her anguish. He runs from her into the garden where he finds the Child drowned in the fountain and the Boy looking maniacally at his drowned sister in the fountain. The Stepdaughter bends protectively over the dead Child as the Boy's suicidal shot takes his life. Some actors affirm that he is dead; others that it is merely acting. The Manager curses his loss of a whole day "over these people."

Six Characters in Search of an Author

Father is a pompous, self-righteous, tormented man with poor judgment about himself as well as others. He married a woman because she was simple, only to find that he couldn't bear neither her company nor her lackluster intellect. He then shifted her off to his secretary. The newly created couple found it necessary to move away because they feared the Father had too much interest in the little daughter.

Mother loves her children, but she longs most for the one who will not accept her, the Son whom the Father took from her soon after he was born. He has grown up without a mother.

Stepdaughter is not really a stepdaughter, but apparently the product of the Mother's marriage to the Father's secretary. After her father, the secretary, dies, she must work for Madame Pace to maintain the family.

Son is tormented by now being attached to anyone. Father has ignored him and sent Mother away with another husband. He insists that he has nothing to do with any of it. He doesn't, but he cannot escape the family.

Boy has been deprived of his place in the family by their going to live with the Father and the Son. Stepdaughter is usually annoyed with him, Mother ignores him in her effort to win the Son, and Father does not seem to know he exists.

The **Child** is loved most by Stepdaughter who tries to comfort her, knowing of course as a character that Little Girl will drown in the fountain.

The Manager is overbearing and slow-witted. He play's the role of the author, but is constrained by his adhearance to his notions of stagecraft.

Madame Pace is the Step-Daughter's madame. She has guilted the Step-Daughter into employment and speaks a comical broken-english.

The Prompter is a member of the crew. At one point he attempts to transcribe the Characters' actions.

The Actors (Leading Lady, Leading Man, Second Lady, Juvenile Lead) are all stereotypical in their roles, and all possess the sentiment that they as actors are better suited to tell the story of the characters' lives than the characters themselves.

CRITICAL VIEWS ON
Six Characters in Search of an Author

ANNE PAOLUCCI ON PIRANDELLO'S EXPLORATION OF THEATER AS A MEDIUM

[Anne Paolucci, for many years Chair of the English Department at St. John's University, has published extensively on Dante as well as Pirandello. In 1974, Pirandello's *Theater, the Recovery of the Modern Stage for Dramatic Art*, was published by the Southern Illinois University Press. In 1986, President Reagan appointed her to a six-year term with the National Council on the Humanities; she remained in this position through the terms of Presidents Bush and Clinton. She has been on the Board of Trustees of The City University of New York since 1996, and was made Chair of that Board in 1997, the first woman to hold that office.]

When, in 1923, at the age of 56, Luigi Pirandello won European acclaim with the Pitoëff production of *Six Characters in Search of an Author* (the same play that had been booed and had caused a riot at its premiere in Rome two years earlier), the Italian writer had already published six of his seven novels, several scattered volumes of short stories, and four volumes of poetry. His reputation as a writer of fiction was already established when he turned to drama; and although he never gave up writing novels and short stories (and was to convert many of these into plays in the years that followed), Pirandello had clearly shifted his sights and direction by 1923. For the rest of his life his artistic priorities were to be focused on theater. (...)

As a playwright, however, Pirandello soon hit on a new and powerful theme, perhaps the inevitable result of focusing on the barren lives of people living in a barren place, where nature itself is hostile and the individual a victim without reprieve. His earliest plays as well as his novels and short stories examined the effect of such an existence in the most detailed way; but by 1921, with *Six Characters*, he turned with even greater fascination to exploring *personality* in its conscious and deliberate effort to come to terms with the environment. We see in *Six Characters* a new obsession translated powerfully into a stage language itself new and overwhelming. (...)

The "theater" plays announce this new and exciting direction in the most vivid terms; and they make clear at the same time that the search for identity was a most promising subject for the new drama of existential emotions and avant-garde techniques. As Robert Brustein insists, Pirandello hit on something truly extraordinary, for his example served to instruct just about every important playwright of our time.[2] In a rush of inspiration, Pirandello wrote in a short span of four years three of the four plays that were to revolutionize the European and world theater and set it on a new, totally unexpected course for decades to come. In *Six Characters*, *Enrico IV*, and *Each in His Own Way*, Pirandello discovered not only his own potential as a playwright but in the process also rediscovered the full potential of theater. Drama, he made stunningly clear, was a *continuum*, a constant *becoming*. He used telescopic techniques to destroy the passive notion of static "illusion" on stage, superimposing action, moving actors in and out of their "formal" roles, juxtaposing "real" events with stage plot, creating a dialectic spiraling of roles within roles, settings within settings, realities within realities. In the fragmentation that resulted, a new force was unleashed that was to revitalize both drama and fiction in the years that followed.

The first large indication of Pirandello's growing interest in exploring the inner world of personality as it seeks organic identity is to be found in the early novel *Il Fu Mattia Pascal* (*The Late Mattia Pascal*), written in 1904. (...)

The people he draws for us are caught in political realities not very different from the Camus-like trap in which Mattia Pascal or the mad emperor Enrico IV find themselves. Even "out of sequence," *I Vecchi e i giovani* is surprisingly consistent with Pirandello's later works in depicting the struggle between oppression and freedom, the search for identity, the existential frustrations and despair in the face of unrelenting hostile forces.

It is indeed in the strange story of Mattia Pascal, however, that Pirandello's exploration of the stages of consciousness and the search for identity is given unexpectedly mature form at a very early date. Escape and return here become a spiraling dialectic, the end circling back to the beginning in a tragic–ironic–humorous conclusion. The protagonist of this early novel has been called "a fugitive from life"[4] but he is more properly a magician creating his own illusions and, as always in Pirandello, rejecting those illusions in the end. The story contains elements of gross improbability, but Pirandello somehow makes it believable. Mattia Pascal, seeking an opportunity to vacation alone and escape his wife's nagging, goes to Monte Carlo, where he wins a great deal of money. On his way home, he reads an account of his "death"—a suicide by drowning, the body identified as his by his wife and others. He accepts this grotesque turn of events as a sign, an opportunity to start a new life. Under the assumed name of Adriano Meis, he proceeds to travel throughout northern Italy; but in time he is once again caught in the familiar web of personal relationships and social commitments and thus realizes that he cannot really ever escape. The new life he has given himself is not only similar to the old but adds to his difficulties, since his new identity cannot be legally recognized. With the realization that he has in fact created a new trap for himself, he stages a second "suicide"— leaving his hat, cane, and a signed note on a parapet of a bridge along the Tiber—and returns to his home in Sicily. There he finds his "widow" married again and with a new family. Not fazed by the problems created by his return (not the least of which is the illegitimate status of his former wife's child by her new husband), he returns to his job as town librarian and dedicates himself to writing about his experience. (...)

Il Fu Mattia Pascal was the first direct statement of a theme rooted in a pessimistic view of man trapped by hostile forces but rising out of that condition by a slowly evolving consciousness of freedom—a theme richly suggesting a cyclical return to a basically unchanged beginning, which is to say, the dialectic of escape and return with all its ironic suggestivity, roles within roles, ironic parallels often superimposed (the first accidental "suicide" and the deliberately staged "suicide"), a special brand of humor (the perverse decision at the end not to cancel the "death certificate"), paradoxes (committing "suicide" in order to be restored to life), multi-layered self-evaluations and self-analyses, restructuring past events according to one's ideal vision or deliberate re-interpretation or some master plan (including the writing of the experience after settling back in), etc.

With *Six Characters* the focus shifts: the core story becomes a distant motif, an echo, a reminder that all experience must pass through the mirror of the self and must be evaluated in terms of that mirror image. The shift can surely be attributed to some extent to the demands of the stage, which—for Pirandello—was the ideal medium for bringing together the illusion of life and the reality of the self. In this play "escape" also becomes freedom from the predictable connection between intentions and deeds: freedom from stage conventions, dramatic action and resolution, familiar dialogue and internal communications. There is nothing uncertain about this first "theater" play; it too is a fully mature product, an incredible tour-de-force, an experiment that could not have been foreseen but would never be forgotten. It marks the beginning of the contemporary theater with all its fragmented attitudes, states of mind, contradictory emotions, Hamlet-like irrelevancies; but little of what follows in other parts of the world will match the totality of the Pirandello experiment. (...)

Così è (*se vi pare*) is the brilliant prelude to the "theater" plays, the first Eisensteinian superimposition of identities. The transformations described in the earlier *Il Fu Mattia Pascal*, within a narrative structure, here are given immediacy on stage as shifting images.(...)

The "theater" plays are proof of the symbiosis achieved. *Six Characters* is a moving stage image of shifting roles in the process of definition: actors playing "real" people, actors playing "actors" in rehearsal; actors creating a new script given to them by the "real" people; life drama measured against the written script of a play; the illusion of improvisation on stage; the core story of passionate and unacceptable emotions narrated by the "real" people who are looking for the perfect "script" in which to relate that story (a story that, in what will become typical Pirandellian fashion, will be truncated by an unexpected event and not brought to traditional dramatic resolution). In this work, Pirandello transforms the stage itself into a multi-layered experience, pushing the dramatic action into the background as he probes the intricate nuances of the role/character relationship and the difficulty of communicating life as drama. The play in fact is a forceful statement of what will become for theater of the "Absurd" one of its most provocative features: theater pushed to the edge of non-theater as its lines of communication break down under the exacting scrutiny of the dramatist-analyst.

NOTES

2. Robert Brustein, "Pirandello's Drama of Revolt," in *Pirandello: A Collection of Critical Essays*, ed. Glauco Cambon (Englewood Cliffs, NJ, 1967), p. 133.

4. Douglas Radcliff-Umstead, *The Mirror of Our Anguish: A Study of Luigi Pirandello's Narrative Writings* (Cranbury, NJ, and London, 1978), p. 162.

—Anne Paolucci, "Sicilian Themes and the Restructured State: The Dialectic of Fiction and Drama in the Work of Luigi Pirandello," *Modernism is European Drama: Ibsen, Strindberg, Pirandello, Beckett. Essays from Modern Drama*, eds. Frederick J. Marker and Christopher Innes (University of Toronto Press, 1998): 170–79.

ANNA BALAKIAN ON SURREALISM IN PIRANDELLO'S DRAMA

[Anna Balakian, formerly chairperson of the Department of Comparative Literature at New York University, has written on Pirandello and is the author of *Snowflake on the Belfry: Dogma and Disquietude in the Critical Arena, Fiction of the Poet: from Mallarme to the Post-Symbolist Mode, Literary Origins of Surrealism, Surrealism: The Road to the Absolute*, and other works of literary criticism.]

An affinity has often been seen between the theater of Pirandello and the surrealist mode because both adhere to such notions as the "absurd," the unconventional, the iconoclastic, and the shocking to stir the receivers of the created work. Let us examine these elements from the angle of Pirandello's *Six Characters in Search of an Author* as well as of the surrealists' position, to determine the nature of affiliations and of differences.

Undeniably, his reception in Paris had much to do with Pirandello's subsequent fame. He wrote *Six Characters* in 1921, but it was not until the play was presented in Paris in 1923 that notoriety was accompanied by sincere curiosity and serious appraisal. Apparently, the influence of innovations is more dramatic when it crosses national frontiers than within a national literature. (...)

Curiously, France, the country historically noted for generating avant-gardism in poetry and painting, was rather slow in its renovation of the theater. (...)

The most popular, prolific, and durable theater was still that of the boulevards' romantic boudoir triangles, the psychological plays of Ibsen and of his followers, or the social theater of François de Curel or Henri Brieux, or even the surviving naturalist theater of Henri Becque. All of these works may have developed fresh insights on humanity and society, but they did not offer fresh, unpredictable forms of representation in the script or new presentations on the stage. (...)

When *Six Characters* hit Paris, surrealism was not yet officially declared, although André Breton and his colleagues were pondering what artistic forms their revolution was to promote. Dada had made its official arrival in Paris in 1920 but had identified with no special art form; collage and theatrical improvisations were fragmentary and meant to be executed or performed before randomly selected audiences. Neither the authors nor the viewers took these shows as dramatic structures. What interested the Dadas and the rising coterie of surrealism in the dramatic form was dialogue, which was viewed as a form of linguistic ping-pong with no special consequence for dramatic action: two streams of thought, two soliloquies interrupting each other rather than responding logically to each other, their incongruities often revealing underlying hostilities in the interlocutors. (...)

The surrealists did not probe or even evoke the questions that touch theater art integrally. In fact, these issues were totally ignored as they would be by people who are unversed; these people, however, were supremely versed and thereby knew what they were destroying, as was the case with Pirandello. In relation to the spectators, what the surrealists hoped to do was to raise the level of imaginative power, but they did not have in mind any specific creation regarding the interplay between author and producer, or actor and audience, at least not until Antonin Artaud's *The Theater and Its Double*, which proposed theatrical devices affecting audience behavior. But Artaud's treatise, which he really did not implement, is posterior to *Six Characters*, which contains both thesis and praxis within a single work.

When we look at *Six Characters* from the point of view of this cursory description of the salient characteristics of fragmental surrealist plays, the differences are jarring. First, Pirandello came to his rebellion as a theatrical craftsman who had mastered conventional theater. He was a professional who wanted to break the rules and not an amateur who knew no better. The impact of the aberration of form becomes much more notable when it is willed and when the rejection or negation carries the weight of new values. Pirandello's flaunting of the rules had affirmative intentions. When in the beginning of the play he has the Director telling his crew that they have to use Pirandello's plays because there is a sudden dearth of plays coming from Paris, he is expressing Pirandello's exasperation with the state of the theater. A few minutes later the characters are telling the Director the reason for their orphaned state: "He [the author] abandoned us in a fit of depression, of disgust for the ordinary theater as the public knows it and likes it," ... is the way the Stepdaughter explains why the characters were abandoned.

Pirandello dissects the theater to find out what ails it. He wants to break down the barriers between generator, director, performer, and receiver (audience). In contrast, the surrealists wanted to break down the divisions between the genres; for them theater was nothing more than an oral poem. (...)

For the surrealist there is no discrete separation between the poetic and the dramatic forms. Poetry includes all the others, which the surrealists are ready to mutate or even mutilate if they can thereby enhance the power of poetry and extend its domain. Pirandello wants to break down the rules the better to preserve the theater. What does he do in *Six Characters* in his effort to strengthen what he considers to be a debilitated form? He is questioning the problem of survival and reality. The first premise is that the work has more chance of survival than its author. "Man, the writer ... the instrument of creation will die. But what is created by him will never die" (Father, Act I). This thought had already been the matrix of the symbolist aesthetics. But once the work attains its independence from the author, it is in turn prone to mutability because it will have to combat and resist other factors endangering its integrity as it gets to mean different things to successive audiences. But unlike the late twentieth-century Derridian "différance" which relates to the privileged reader's inclinations to change the meaning of a text, that of the theater performance is more vulnerable. It is subjected to a triple tier of interpretation because it has to go through the process of its theatricalization in the hands first of the director, second of the actors, and only finally of the audience.

So, in truth the fate of this created reality (which is presumably "fixed") is as precarious as that of the human one. If human reality is ephemeral because of the impact of time, which turns today's reality into a yesterday no more substantial than an illusion, the theatrical reality that we call illusion and that at first glance seems impermeable to the ravages of human time, is just as vulnerable because of the future impact of rethinking on the part of producers, performers, and the changing responses of succeeding audiences. (...)

In the case of *Six Characters*, the question of viability becomes even more complicated because at a certain junction reality intervenes to destroy illusion. Or in other words a real-life event—the actual drowning of a little girl and the suicide of the boy—brings art and reality into collision, violating the created reality of the fixed characters. They cannot be represented if they no longer exist. The play is pulverized before the very eyes of those who want to perform lit. However relative truth may be and however dependent reality may be on point of view, these become totally academic problems as soon as the created reality disintegrates. The conclusion of the problmatics of the creative process, which is the center of Pirandello's preoccupation, is a state of nihilism. It takes on a more concrete form in the idiotic laughter with which the play ends in the definitive version of the script. This is not the laughter of effervescence we sometimes meet in surrealist expression. (...)

The primordial process of theater was and always has been the representation of life, and the creation of illusion has been only a means of reinforcing that reality. The indeterminacy of reality in the modern world made the normal process of creating that no longer reliable. Pirandello leaves us with the picture of the artist finding his art inadequate and revealing the quagmire through the deterioration of the medium. To his viewers the image of the disintegration of theater became a source of new freedom for the art. By letting the audience share his secret, Pirandello revealed to himself as well as to the adept viewer an infinite number of new channels open to theater.

Pirandello's efforts at philosophizing were expressed in the discourse of his play, but the form in which this discourse was couched proved to have more substantive value and more impact on the future of theater than the content of that discourse. He had unwittingly liberated the structure of theater for the rest of the century. A seeming informality in stage-craft opened the possibilities of audience involvement; plot irresolution became acceptable, and the curtain separating illusion from reality vanished. If the freedom of the characters from their author's intentions was already an impudent step, an even more far-reaching break in the definitive version of the play occurred when Pirandello's stage directions bid the characters to burst into the arena of the audience. (...)

By deconstructing the mechanism of theater, Pirandello was able to demonstrate which of the elements were trappings and which were the essentials. By having the author challenged by the producer (or in the more appropriate French word the "réalisateur"), Pirandello launched in Europe the era of the great impresarios who gave their own imprints to a play and even in some cases managed to give cohesion to some loosely constructed ones. In a subsequent age, which did not produce great drama, the permissibility practiced by this new breed of directors made it possible for playwrights such as Thornton Wilder to endow drama with a certain contrived informality, giving the director more opportunity to exercise his own creativity.

—Anna Balakian, "Pirandello's *Six Characters and Surrealism*," *A Companion to Pirandello Studies* (Greenwood Press, 1991): 185–92.

EMMANUELA TANDELLO ON PIRANDELLO'S INFLUENCE ON STOPPARD

[Emmanuela Tandello is Lecturer in Italian at University College, London. In addition to her writing on Pirandello, she is on the editorial board of the Pirandello Society and *The Yearbook of the Pirandello Society*. She has also written on Tom Stoppard and Amelia Rosselli.]

Tom Stoppard has claimed that any pirandellian 'presence' recognisable in his work should not be considered as proof of direct literary influence, but rather as evidence of the generalised 'impossibility' for any contemporary Western playwright 'to write a play that is totally unlike Beckett, Pirandello, Kafka...'[2] (...)

Whilst stressing that all of Stoppard's plays reveal such traits, to a greater or lesser extent, Lepschy identifies *Rosencrantz and Guildenstern are Dead* [from now on abbreviated as R&G] as the play which most clearly and forcefully shares themes and predicaments with some of Pirandello's best known texts, namely *Sei personaggi in cerca d'autore* and *Enrico IV*. This study fully supports and develops this view. In offering a 'pirandellian' reading of the structure of this play, I hope to show how Stoppard's 'theatrical manifesto', the text that more than any other establishes 'the rules of the game he intends to play with theatre'[6] develops pirandellian themes such as *fissità* and the metadrama of creativity to a high degree of sophistication and skill; and how such complexity can indeed reflect back on those very themes, and on Pirandello's own metadramatic texts in a mutually enlightening relationship. (...)

R&G is, from its very genesis, and notwithstanding its undeniably comic, slapstick manner, both a tragedy of characters and a drama of creativity, and therefore an exercise in metatheatre in the pirandellian sense of the word. The two literary characters Stoppard chooses as the protagonists of his play stand at the convergence of different texts, scripts as well as productions, which have made them (...)

belong to a theatrical tradition, which endorses limitations and lack of characterisation by nicknaming them 'knife and fork', and sometimes excluding them from the script altogether. (...)

As characters, they fulfil a theatrical 'function' for which development of personality, from the point of view of the playwright, is pointless; at the same time, they are 'caught in the act', or in the script, which is being written by someone else— not merely Shakespeare (or Pirandello), but indeed Hamlet (or Enrico), 'main' characters who, unlike them, are at liberty, to a certain extent, to 'choose' and construct their own script, and as a consequence determine everybody else's behaviour. This is the truth that Ros and Guil have to face in the end, (...)

having failed to produce their own alternative script, and having to accept theatrical death as their only 'life'. (...)

Stoppard, like Pirandello, spots a dramatic potential that allows him to make a statement about reality through a statement about the theatre (and the other way round). (...)

Like Pirandello, he places the idea of the *fissità* of the characters firmly at the centre of his play, as its unshakeable, irrefutable truth. And in doing so, he plays the two characters a nasty trick:

> GUIL: We are not restricted. No boundaries have been defined, no inhibitions imposed ... Spontaneity and whim are the order of the day. Other wheels are turning but they are not our concern. We can breathe. We can relax. We can do what we like and say what we like to whomever we like, without restriction. (...)

Their impression of freedom, deriving from the new 'space', the hypothetical 'new life' afforded them by the second author, is constantly thwarted, and disproved, by their inability not to become 'caught up' in the script they should ideally be avoiding. As William Babula reminds us, 'the artists [both Shakespeare and Stoppard] have played a cruel joke on Ros and Guil.' (...)

I said earlier that Stoppard takes pirandellian fixity to extremes of sophistication—the finality of the script, in his play, is above all that of the Shakespearean text which it manipulates. If the characters are caught in it, so is he as author. (...)

All of Pirandello's texts concerned with the existence of the literary character as an entity, indeed a creature with a life that is independent of authorial intention, rely on one vital (in the strictest sense of the word) ambiguity. The literary character does not need an author, nor indeed a text, to 'exist'—but its lack of form or development depends on both author and text for its aesthetic realisation. (...)

The presence of the script is therefore central to their predicament: it is their only hope, but also their damnation. If the 'imagination' of the author has frozen them into an eternal formlessness, their (his) script will both 'give them life' and fix them forever. The 'momento eterno' so feared by the Father is indeed the moment of writing, which will seal his fate and fix him 'in quel solo momento fuggevole e vergognoso' of his life. Yet, the centrality of the script can only by proven by assuming, or suggesting its fictitious absence within the play. In *Sei personaggi* Pirandello explores the ambiguity in the life of the literary character by apparently denying them textual life altogether. The Father affirms his and the others' existence despite the 'absence' of 'un copione che ci contenga', character, without a script, not without an author, given that an author did beget them. (...)

And in fact, the idea of the author in the play is dropped, as the characters claim their own potentiality as 'text' ('potremmo essere noi la loro nuova commedia'), and proceed to reassure the Capocomico that there is no need for anybody to 'write' it, but only to 'transcribe' it. (...)

The characters are given a chance to write their own script, given the freedom of movement and choice. But this is yet another device on Pirandello's part, which hides the author's anxiety and fears–the chance for each individual character to voice a point of view, to tell the story in his or her own way does not, in the end, prevent any of them from being forever fixed in their role. Two well-known devices are at play here: the 'play within the play' and the 'play in the making'. Both allow the playwright to reintroduce authorship into his text whilst pretending to be holding back. By having the characters exist with(out) the script: that is to say, within it as a potentiality, and with(out) it as the condition of its coming into being, by allowing them to exist at the convergence of these two different textual spaces, to constantly cross the threshold between their drama and the script (in Stoppard-like terms, we could call them their 'on stage' and 'off stage' moments) as they both perform and comment on their roles, (...)

the playwright constructs his *own* play (the one on the characters' predicament). The gain, for the characters, is immortality, their loss, immutability. The script is written, nothing can be done. Their fate is sealed forever, and the playwright's anxiety of creation (temporarily) released. (...)

Dramatic action in R&G develops (...)

between a script that is acknowledged in the title of the play itself ('Rosencrantz and Guildenstern are dead' is indeed a line from *Hamlet*) and by the audience, the playwright and some of the characters—and a script 'in the making', which Ros and Guil, temporarily freed of their identity by the new space opened for them by the playwright between 'acts', are unable to 'write'. We have, in other words, two characters existing, like Pirandello's, both within and with(out) a script—but the levels of interaction are far more complex than in the starkly polarised situation of Pirandello's plays. The main difference with Pirandello's characters is Ros and Guil's lack of awareness both as characters and as personae. Ros and Guil are not merely trying to recover textual memory, they are trying to construct it—but their task is made far more complicated by the number of scripts with which they interact, and by the different levels at which they are required to operate. (...)

Again, the difference with Pirandello lies in the multiplication of the polarised situation of *Sei personaggi*. The characters are made to operate between the potential script (the new play) and the virtual script (the 'old' play). They are assigned an existence with (out) the latter through the device of the on stage/off stage moments; but they are deliberately not allowed to exist fully within the new script. (...)

Ros and Guil reach the realisation of the impossibility to depart from the original script and their destiny at the same time as the playwright—the whole play has been a converging on our little deaths'. They die, and the playwright can do nothing but allow the logic of the text to take its course, because 'in one sense they have failed to do more than improvise dialogue and stage business'. As minor characters, they have been proved incapable—in pirandellian terms, they have been proven 'unfinished', 'incomplete'—to sustain the role of protagonists.

NOTES

2. *Behind the Scenes: Theatre and Film Interviews from the Transatlantic Review*, edited by J. F. McCrindle, with an introduction by J. V. Van Italie (London: Pitman, 1971), p. 83.

6. R. Gordon, *cit.* p. 17

—Emmanuela Tandello, "Characters With(out) a Text: Script as Destiny in Stoppard and Pirandello," *The Yearbook of the Society for Pirandello Studies* 13: 35–45.

JEROME MAZZARO ON INFLUENCES ON PIRANDELLO

[Jerome Mazzaro was Professor of Modern Languages and Literatures for over 30 years at the University of Buffalo. In his prolific career, he has published numerous essays on Pirandello's work. He is also the author of *Transformations in the Renaissance English Lyric* (Cornell University Press, 1970) and *William Carlos Williams: The Later Poems* (Cornell University Press, 1973).]

Comparisons between Luigi Pirandello's *Sei personaggi in cerca d'autore* (*Six Characters in Search of an Author*, 1921, 1925) and Greek tragedy are common, with *Sei personaggi* representing "modern" or "contemporary" tragedy, and, indeed, it would seem that the drama's world-view resembles that described by Rachel Bespaloff and George Dimock for Homeric epic upon which many of the Greek tragedies are based. Bespaloff's view of the Homeric gods as the cause of everything that happens and as taking no responsibility and the epic heroes as taking "total responsibility even for that which they have not caused" is certainly applicable to Pirandello's "characters" who, in trying to survive in a world not of their creation, take responsibility for those drives that make possible their survival.[1] However, in so doing, rather than take on the world-view and values of a Zeus-centered cosmos, they take on the values of a world ruled by a Prime Mover who, in the words of Friedrich Nietzsche, is dead and whose accredited dogmas in science and religion are, as, David Hilbert and Matthew Arnold indicate, under assault. (...)

The "absolutes"of *Sei personaggi* are (...)

internal, rooted, as Adriano Tilgher [has] argued (...)

in a dualism of life and form. They arise either as individual or social psychologically defining moments out of which compulsively repetitious actions emanate or as "rocklike memories" which, in the words of Robert Lowell, fix "in the mind, where [they] survive all the distortions of fantasy ... [and] blank befogging of forgetfulness" or as "masks" forcefully or voluntarily imposed on one.[4] They become the expressive forms to which subjective impulses aspire and which presumably are the discoveries of authors who, in the manner of Freud's "Creative Writers and Daydreaming" (1908), alter and disguise the character of egoistic daydreams and gain acceptance through purely formal or aesthetic yields of pleasure or, as Pirandello says in "The New Theatre and the Old" (1922) and T. S. Eliot in "Tradition and the Individual Talent" (1917), succeed through "disinterestedness" and "the extinction of personality" in creating a voice that sounds to whoever hears it as their own. What the drama lacks, according to both its title and "Preface," is an internal author to give the characters' actions unity and design. "Their play does not manage to get presented," Pirandello says, "precisely because the author whom they seek is missing." (...)

Nonetheless, for defenders of the work, the absence of an internal author in no way means that there is no author. There is Pirandello, who is outside the action in the selection and arrangement of incidents and in the drama's extensive stage directions, "indifferent" and, as James Joyce's says of the artist, "paring his fingernails."[6] (...)

In *Sei personaggi* there are three ongoing voices or actions. There are the narrative of the characters' lives, the efforts of the actors and the Manager to turn this narrative into the conventions of theater, and the authorial control of these two contexts to manage a work of art. The first voice is, as Umberto Mariani says, "an old-fashioned tearjerker ... typical of the bourgeois theater" and involving the kind of material "that Pirandello rejected from the very beginning of his career as a playwright."[8] Of itself this material is not the basis of enduring art, and one can understand the author's willingness to abandon characters associated with it. It is, however, what the public sees and likes. The second voice provides the drama's comic element and is reflective, if not of Karl Marx's observation that the second time historical events occur, they do so as farce, then of Friedrich Schlegel's sense of "perpetual irony" or "transcendental farce" in an artist's dominating his subject matter by choosing not to take it seriously or Pascal's and Henri Bergson's seeing laughter in duplication and mechanical repetition.[9] With its inclusion not only of the "miracle" materialization of Madame Pace but also of mysterious lighting effects and the dreamlike appearance of the Father, the Mother, and the Son on stage at the drama's close, the final voice is the most troubling, for it appears to sacrifice psychological and aesthetic considerations for "spiritual" or "transcendent forces operative in the universe that defy human comprehension and logic" and troubles efforts at rational interpretation. It is this voice which Pirandello then contradicts in his own productions by emphasizing the drama's psychological and aesthetic elements and suggesting a Creator who is omnipresent and unseen and who, like the author, has set his handiwork "adrift upon the uncertain sea of existence."[10] (...)

With his voices, Pirandello is able to conceive in *Sei personaggi* a drama about the writing of a drama and to invent what Wylie Sypher calls "cubist drama."[11] Audiences no longer see by means of illusion so much as *into* illusion. Plot as it pertains to linear development becomes subordinate to life and art exchanges, and the stage curtain which had once served to separate them disappears for most of the performance. A density or opacity emerges that intensifies the spell of drama at the same time that theater's traditional devices of exit and closure are weakened. Internal deconstruction becomes an issue which in *Sei personaggi* Pirandello tries to solve by abandonment or exhaustion. (...)

Gaspare Giudice is willing to postpone these questions to promote the drama's advances and propose that the problems that critics have in accepting *Sei personaggi* lie not in "failed poetic clarity, but rather in the sense of a crystallized poetry of ambiguity." He attributes this ambiguity to the drama's having originated in what Pirandello in its "Preface" calls "a spontaneous illumination" and to the playwright's having "limited himself to *assisting* and to making sure that the values of the *vision* prevailed in the theatrical record that he was writing of it." (...)

Even if one agrees with Giudice that the origin of *Sei personaggi* lies in a visionary experience, one has a recognizable history leading to that vision. Critics note foreshadowings of the drama and its themes in such diverse works as "La tragedia di un personaggio" (1911) and "Colloqui coi personaggi" (1915), the novels *Il fu Mattia Pascal* (1904) and *Si gira* (1916), the dramas *Così è (se vi pare)* and *Il giuoco delle parti*, and various critical writings including those he did for newspapers.[15] As early as 1904, he had written to a friend that if conditions permitted, he would sit in his study all day "at the service of characters, who crowded around him, ... each one with his particular unhappiness to make public." He makes specific mention of the action that centers *Sei personaggi* in a second letter, this one written in 1917 to his son Stefano. He calls the action "a novel to be composed" and describes it as "six characters in a terrible situation" who came to him to be put in a novel. He wants to have nothing to do with their obsession and chases them away. In the end, the novel will turn out to be the encounter, its effects, and his refusal. Not yet determined, Olga Ragusa notes, are the action's theatrical potential, its division of the author into the play's Manager and acting company, and the revised ending confounding art and life which Pirandello settled on in 1925 and which seems to have benefitted from his own ongoing interest in creativity and the innovative productions of the drama's 1921 version by Georges Pitoëff in Paris and Max Reinhardt in Berlin. By Pirandello's own admission, World War I "revealed" his theatrical talents. When the conflicting passions it aroused "were unleashed [he] made [his] creatures suffer [those] passions on the stage as a means of exploration and purgation. (...)

No doubt, as with Pirandello's other works, autobiographical elements are likewise present, especially, since, as Ragusa says, despite statements to the contrary, there is often "no clear break between the manner in which [Pirandello] himself experienced the world and the manner in which his fictional figures experience it." (...)

As with any innovative work, revisions in the two major versions of *Sei personaggi* tend to bring into better inner consistency and balance a number of elements. The changes sharpen and clarify the oppositions necessary to understand the drama's tensions of life and art. They turn talk into action and telling into showing, and they use more effectively the theater's resources, pushing them into rarely if ever previously trafficked areas. In some instances, they also improve the logic and order of events. Cut from the original version is the Father's long speech in Act I which summarizes the events of the characters' lives and foretells the drama's eventual resolution. Likewise cut is the Son's speech near the beginning of Act II recounting his forced recognition at some vague time of his parents' sexual lives and a long exchange between the Father and the Manager early in Act III, in which the Father links man's reasoning and introspective qualities to suffering and man's eagerness to get at the cause of his sufferings. Transposed are the attempted reconciliation between the Mother and the Son and the Stepdaughter's moving speech to her young sister. Both move from Act II to Act III and in the revised version appear in a reverse order. Added are a new beginning and end, new stage and costuming directions, new lighting instructions, new stage blocking, and a "Preface" which evolved out of lectures that Pirandello delivered to audiences after performances of the play. The revisions have also been explained in terms of external forces: Pirandello's adjusting to the criticism of his work by Tilgher, audience reactions, reaction to different productions of the work, and reactions to his exposures to theatrical production and theory and perhaps the writings of the Russian Nikolai Evreinov.[19]

NOTES

1. Rachel Bespaloff, *On the Iliad*, trans. Mary McCarthy (1947; rpt. New York: Harper, 1962), pp. 73–74; George E. Dimock, Jr., "The Name of Odysseus," *Hudson Review*, 9 (1956), 52–70, It should be pointed out that the

1921 and 1925 texts of *Sei personaggi* have significant differences and the version most common in English is based on the 1921 text. This essay uses primarily the 1925 revision, published at Florence by R. Bemporal.

4. Adriano Tilgher, "Life versus Form," trans. Glauco Cambon, in *Pirandello: A Collection of Critical Essays*, ed. Glauco Cambon (Englewood Cliffs: Prentice-Hall, 1967), pp. 19–34; Robert Lowell, *Life Studies* (New York: Farrar, Straus and Cudahy, 1:959), pp. 12–13.

6. James Joyce, *A Portrait of the Artist as a Young Man*, ed. J. S. Atherton (London: Heinemann, 1964), p. 199.

8. Umberto Mariani, "'The Delusion of Mutual Understanding': Structure, Language and Meaning in *Six Characters*," in *A Companion to Pirandello Studies*, ed. DiGaetani, p. 195.

9. Karl Marx, "The Eighteenth Brumaire of Louis Napoleon," in *Selected Writings*, ed. C. P. Dutt (New York: International Publishers, n.d.), II, 315, and Henri Bergson, *Laughter*, trans. Cloudesley Brereton and Fred Rothwell (New York: Macmillan, 1911). Pirandello cites Schlegel in his *On Humor*, trans. Antonio Illiano and Daniel P. Testa (Chapel Hill: Univ. of North Carolina Press, 1974), p. 7.

10. A. Richard Sogliuzzo, *Luigi Pirandello, Director* (Metuchen, N.J.: Scarecrow Press, 1982), p. 151.

11. Wylie Sypher, "Cubist Drama," in *Pirandello*, ed. Cambon, pp. 67–71.

15. Emanuele Licastro, *Luigi Pirandello dalle novelle alle commedie* (Verona: Fiorini, 1974), pp. 35–36; Olga Ragusa, *Luigi Pirandello* (Edinburgh: Edinburgh Univ. Press, 1980), pp. 140–42.

19. For similarities between Pirandello's and Evreinov's views, see Olle Hildebrand, "Pirandello's Theater and the Influence of Nicolai Evreinov," *Italica*, 60 (Summer 1983), 107–39, and Tony Pearson, "Evreinov and Pirandello: Two Theatricalists in Search of the Chief Thing," *Theatre Research International*, 17 (Spring 1992), 26–38. In 1925, Pirandello staged two of Evreinov's plays. See also Olga Ragusa's discussion of Pirandello's revisions to *Sei personaggi* in her *Luigi Pirandello: An Approach to His Theatre* (Edinburgh: Edinburgh Univ. Press, 1989), pp. 137–46; "Teaching *Six Characters*," *Teaching Language Through Literature*, 24, No. 2 (April 1985), 3–14; and "*Six Characters*, 1921–25 and Beyond," *Pirandello 1986*, ed. Gian Paolo Biasin and Nicolas J. Perella (Rome: Bulzoni, 1987), pp. 19–30.

—Jerome Mazzaro, "Pirandello's Sei Personaggi and Expressive Form," *Comparative Drama* 30: 4 (1996–97): 503–24

URSULA FANNING ON MALE USURPATION OF FEMALE ROLES

[Ursula Fanning is Professor of Italian at the University College Dublin. In addition to her work on Pirandello, she has recently published *Woman As Subject in the Fictional Universe of Matilde Serao* (Irish Academic Press, 2001)]

Adultery is omnipresent in Pirandello.[1] (...)

It is worth pausing at the beginning of this investigation to consider exactly what it is that we understand by adultery. Maggie Günsberg makes the point, in her excellent work on Pirandello, that the term 'adultery' itself originally referred only to wives and not husbands, in so far as it considered in 'a wife's granting of marital advantages 'to another' rather than to their owner, her husband'.[3] This, indeed, is the adulterous triangle to which Pirandello devotes most space in these plays: husband, wife, wife's lover.

It is, nonetheless, important to point out that the concept of male adultery did exist. Under the Augustan *lex Julia de adulteriis*, of 18 B.C., men could suffer penalties for adultery if they engaged in intercourse with married women, or with unmarried women not of a lower class![4] Medieval churchmen, as Julius Kirshner points out, denounced adulterous husbands quite as much as adulterous wives; such evidence as exists from this period also indicates that medieval courts punished husbands found guilty of adultery.[5] Eva Cantarella stresses, however, that the apparent trend in the nineteenth and early twentieth-century law codes towards a single standard for both sexes is deceptive.[6] Sanctions for unfaithful husbands were different from those for unfaithful wives. (...)

Roman philosophers debated on the adulterous woman at length, concluding that an adulterous woman not only dishonours her husband, but also calls into question the paternity of her sons.[8] The relationship between father and son, rather than father and child, is centralized both by the philosophers and, I suggest, often in the work of Pirandello.[9] (...)

In considering adulterous patterns in these Pirandello plays, we find ourselves inevitably moving towards a consideration of paternal–filial relations. Yet this is not what we initially tend to associate with adultery. Rather, what normally comes to mind on considering adultery are romantic love, lust and passion. Perhaps the most striking element of these Pirandellian plays when one turns to them with the theme of adultery in mind is the absence of lust. Mary Ann Frese Witt has already commented on 'the absence of, or at least the lack of emphasis on, romantic love' in Pirandello's plays.[10] It transpires that not only romantic love, but lust itself is absent from these adulterous scenarios. (...)

Are these plays unusual in their ritual exclusion of any depiction of sexual desire? It seems not. We may remember that in *La morsa* (1898), desire is located outside what we see, in the *antefatto*, before the play starts.[12] What we encounter here are the consequences, rather than the representation, of female adultery. (...)

It may well be that in many Pirandellian plays, as Maggie Günsberg points out, we find 'female sexuality as plot motivator—it precipitates the subsequent action of the play' (Günsberg, p. 10). It is also the case, however, that female desire remains, for Pirandello, unrepresentable.[15] It is, perhaps, simply too disruptive.

It is unlikely that Pirandello shied away from representing female desire in an adulterous context because of censorship, or through any personal sense of moral impropriety. On the contrary, as Giudice tells us, Pirandello liked to use 'lo scandalo come strumento decisivo di espressione', and was proud of the 'audacia' of his theatre.[16] We have also seen in the character of the stepdaughter in *Sei personaggi* that he is well able to represent both sexuality and sensuality—but the step-daughter is precisely a child of adultery and an incestuous object for the father, the actors and the implied audience. She is there to be looked at, not to express any desires of her own. (...)

The experience of the female body is a tale not told by Pirandello. It is equally true, though, that the experiences of the male body remain unnarrated. What is *not* obscured in these plays is the desire of the male characters (be they biological fathers, cuckolds, or both as is the case of the father in *Sei personaggi*) for children. Their desire, in fact, seems to centre wholly on children. Hence, these adulterous plays, contrary to our expectations, are not entirely about men and women: they are at least as concerned with men and children. (...)

Paternal desire is more easily traceable in these plays than erotic desire. (...)

Where does this obsession with paternity come from? Its roots are probably both biographical and cultural. In discussing the biographical dimension of representations of paternity here, I have no wish to indulge in any crude psychologizing of the author. It is, nonetheless, possible to see traces of Pirandello's relationship with his own father, to find what Giudice called 'l'ombra di questo grande padre incurante e prepotente' (Giudice, p. 19) in the conflictual relationships between older and younger men in Pirandello's work.[18] We can also find reflections of Pirandello's own experiences as a father in his depiction of relationships between fathers and children.[19] (...)

It is also likely, however, especially when we think of the terms in which paternity and maternity are presented in *Liolà* that Pirandello is drawing on the, then still widely held, belief that the father is the creative force in the formation of the child. (...)

The anthropologist, Carol Delaney, has examined the meaning of paternity and the cultural beliefs surrounding it. The context of her work is that of Turkey in the mid-1980s, but what she says sheds much light on Pirandello's Sicily in the early years of this century and, indeed, Delaney extrapolates and draws conclusions relevant to contemporary western society on the basis of her findings. (...)

Carol Delaney's research is potentially illuminating for both *Pensaci, Giacomino!* and *Sei personaggi*. This centres on the question of ownership of the child. Delaney notes that, in the context in which she is working: 'men are considered to be the authors/creators of children as God is thought to be the author/creator of the world. Because of this, children belong to their father; they are his seed' (Delaney, p. 5001. This belief underlies crucial elements of both plays. (...)

How does the idea of paternal ownership illuminate *Sei*

personaggi? The naming of characters is clearly significant here. Not only, as Günsberg has said, does the identification of characters favour and centralize the legitimate family (Günsberg, p. 142), with padre, madre and figlio, a clear unit set against figliastra, giovinetto and bambina, but it also seems crucial here that the padre and madre are identified as such rather than as marito and moglie. In other words, our attention is drawn to the parenting functions of these characters. But what kind of parenting functions are they? Despite the fact that the father famously exclaims of the mother 'Non è una donna; è una madre' (*MN* II, p. 62), and goes on to define her drama as consisting in 'questi quattro figli dei due uomini ch'ella ebbe' (*MN* II, p. 62), it is noticeable that these children are defined here as the property of the men concerned. (...)

The negation/usurpation of the maternal role which corresponds to the centralization of the paternal role may be seen as a process of displacement in these plays. Most Pirandellian mothers retreat into silence, (e.g. Mita), non-presence (e.g. Lillina), or virtual incoherence (e.g. the mother in *Sei personaggi*, protesting her linguistic inadequacies).

Pirandello's male characters, in most of the plays considered here, have usurped the role of the mother and taken unto themselves all creative force in the biological realm. But their creative powers are not confined to the biological. Most of them control and, in a sense, create and limit the existences of those around them whatever their marital and paternal status. (...)

It is interesting, in this light, to note that for Pirandello authorship is a form of creation which is essentially maternal. (...)

Pirandello consistently sees writing as a kind of spontaneous generation within the artist who is at once mother and father to his characters (as we have seen his male characters prove to be, often, for their offspring). (...)

These links between men and women (husbands and wives, wives and lovers) in the plays are tenuous in the extreme. I noted at the beginning of this article that Pirandello was most interested in the husband–wife–lover triangle. It would seem more accurate to conclude that Pirandello is interested in the adulterous triangle insofar as it allows him to explore what is a particularly significant dyad for him: that of father and child.

NOTES

1. Examples of this omnipresent theme (other than those I intend to discuss in detail) are to be found in the following plays: *La morsa* [1898] in *Maschere nude* II (Milan, Mondadori, 1961), *Il dovere del medico* [1912] *MN* II, *La ragione degli altri* [1916] in *Maschere nude* I (Milan, Mondadori, 1958), *All'uscita* [1916] *MN* II, *Il piacere dell'onestà* [1918] *MN* I, *Il gioco delle parti* [1919] *MN* I, *L'uomo, la bestia, e la virtù* [1919] *MN* I, *Tutto per bene* [1920] *MN* I, *Come prima, meglio di prima* [1921] *MN* I, *La signora Morli, una e due* [1922] *MN* II, *Diana e la Tuda* [1927] *MN* I, *Bellavita* [1928] *MN* II, *Lazzaro* [1929] *MN* II, *Non si sa come* [1935] *MN* II. From this list, we can see that the theme of adultery was one that held a fascination for Pirandello throughout his writing life. There are other plays in which illegitimate children are of importance, but these illegitimate children cannot properly be called the children of adulterous relationships. I am thinking here, for instance, of plays such as *L'innesto* [1921] and *L'altro figlio* [1925] where the offspring are the result of rape.

3. Maggie Günsberg, *Patriarchal Representations: Gender and Discourse in Pirandello's Theatre*, Oxford, Berg, 1994. All further references are to this edition. The ultimate source of the quotation within this quotation is D. Williman, *Legal Terminology: An Historical Guide to Technical Language of Law*, Canada, Broadview Press, 1986.

4. David Cohen, 'The Augustan Law on Adultery: The Social and Cultural Context' in *The Family in Italy from Antiquity to the Present*, edited by David L. Kertzer and Richard P. Saller, London, Yale University Press, 1991, pp. 109–26 (p. 111). All further references are to this edition.

5. Julius Kirshner, 'Introduction to Part Two' of *The Family in Italy*, pp. 147–49 (p. 148).

6. Eva Cantarella, 'Homicides of Honour: The Development of Italian Adultery Law over Two Millennia' in *The Family in Italy*, pp. 229–44.

8. *Controversiae* (9.1.14, 1.4.12, 7.5.13–15); see Cohen pp. 115–16.

9. There are, of course, important father–daughter relationships dealt with in Pirandello's plays. See, for example, *Tutto per bene* which provides an interesting consideration of what it is to be a father, alongside a typical example of Pirandellian conflict over the paternal role.

10. Mary Ann Frese Witt, 'Woman or Mother? Feminine Conditions in Pirandello's Theatre' in *A Companion to Pirandello Studies*, edited by J. L. DiGaetani, London, Greenwood Press, 1991, pp. 57–72 (p. 57). All further references are to this edition.

12. Luigi Pirandello, *La morsa* [1898] in *MN* II.

15. In *Trovarsi* [1932], Act II (*MN* II), Donata and Elisa discuss female desire at some length. It remains unrepresented.

16. Giovanni Giudice, *Pirandello*, Turin, UTET, 1963, p. 344. All further references are to this edition.

18. See also chapter 6 of Günsberg's work, 'Camaraderie in Competition: Male Bonding and Male Rivalry' (pp. 64–99).

19. Examples include the intense father–son and father–step-daughter relationships in *Sei personaggi*, and the close bond between Toti and Nini in *Pensaci, Giacomino!* I will discuss these in greater detail in the next section of this article.

—Ursula Fanning, "Adultery: The Paternal Potential," *Yearbook for the Society of Pirandello Studies* 15 (1995–1996): 7–17.

J.L. STYAN ON PIRANDELLO'S INNOVATIONS

[J.L. Styan, deceased Franklyn Bliss Snyder Professor Emeritus of English Literature and Theatre at Northwestern University, received his M.A. at Cambridge. He published more than a dozen books on Shakespeare and the drama, including *Shakespeare's Stagecraft* and *The Shakespeare Revolution*. In 1995 he was awarded the Robert Lewis Medal for Lifetime Achievement in Theatre Research.]

Pirandello has a good deal in common with Molière: his results are so thought-provoking that he is discussed first as a philosopher when he is very much of a *farceur*.[1] I have chosen the word carefully, and use it in the sense of "practical joker."[2] And his methods seem to encourage directors to take liberties of their own. Those interested in the story of his success on the stage point to the sensational production of *Six Characters in Search of an Author* when it was directed by Georges Pitoëff at the Théâtre des Champs-Elysées in 1923. By that time the Paris audience was moderately accustomed to the shocks and surprises of a symbolist and surrealist drama. 1917 had seen Apollinaire's *The Breasts of Tiresias*, in which the rebellious feminist wore red and blue balloons for bosoms, and let them fly on strings before exploding them. 1921 saw Cocteau's *The Wedding on the Eiffel Tower*, also at the Théâtre des Champs-Elysées, a play flaunting two music-hall compères dressed as gramophones and a set like a camera: on the command, "Watch the birdie!", an ostrich stepped out.

But in 1923, the actors in *Six Characters* did worse yet: they entered in their everyday clothes and walked through the auditorium. They had invaded the province of the audience, breaking the comfortable rule of nineteenth-century theatre that actors should know their place. And when they climbed on the stage, there was nothing on it. Neither Apollinaire nor Cocteau had thought of being as surrealistic as *that*. Then came the sensation. When it was the moment for the six Characters to enter, they were flooded with a green light and lowered to the stage in an old cage-lift, a stage elevator previously used for scenery. Pitoëff had had a bright idea, Paris went wild, and Pirandello was honored by the French government. (...)

Pirandellian drama was working a fresh vein of theatre, one which would nowadays be explained as "metatheatre": theatre which makes its audience conscious of the theatre's own element in order to work. In *L'umorismo* Pirandello had insisted that comedy must make us "perceive the opposite," and that humor must make us "*feel* the opposite."[5] But in that provocative essay he was writing as a theorist. The problem for Pirandello the practical theatre artist was to find a way to *make* us perceive and feel the opposite. (...)

To make each member of his audience a Pirandellian humorist, he contrived to make us see that the other side of tragedy is farce, that when you have peeled an onion there is nothing left but tears, that a life of chance is a terrifying thing. (...)

Pirandello's theatrical "if" was used like a question mark, Stanislavsky's like a commandment. Pirandello's "if" inspired the conflicting accounts of sanity and insanity in *It Is So!* (*If You Think So*) in 1916—they deceive the audience as much as the townspeople. It inspired his masterpieces, *Six Characters* written in three weeks in 1921, *Henry IV* written in two in 1922. (...)

Like any *farceur*, Pirandello works hard to manipulate the responses of his audience by tricks and surprises. His most successful moments are those when the stage succeeds in asserting total control. In *Six Characters*, one of his concerns is to startle us with the suggestion (later picked up by Harold Pinter) that only creatures of fiction are likely to know what they are. Other people are like Pirandello himself when he noted in horror that "Someone is living my life, and I don't know a thing about him." So he tries to bring his audience to a belief that fictional characters can be more real than live actors, even when the actors apparently belong to our world.

The achievements of the milliner's shop scene lies in that. The fictional Father and Step-daughter are to perform with an Ibsenite earnestness, on the most profound level of realism the players are capable of. Then, "without seeming false in any way," as Pirandello's direction insists, the Leading Man and the Leading Lady are simply to repeat their words. A brilliant device! No matter how well they act, they must *always* seem false. The plain fact is that when you imitate someone, it always sounds as if you are putting him down. And even if the difference is only slight, to perceive it is to be convinced that the copy is wrong. Such inevitability was another of Pirandello's tricks, and the pain of the Father and the Step-daughter had inevitably to give way to laughter.

To top this, Pirandello makes devilish use of the customary prompter of the period, as the revised version of 1925 insists. The Prompter presumably reads all the lines in a high-pitched monotone as if from his box downstage center. The Actors come in a fraction of a second behind him, giving the unreal effect of an echo, thus: "Good afternoon, Miss / afternoon, Miss." Then the Actors say the wretched lines yet again, till all feeling is drained from them. Clearly knowing what he was doing, Pirandello went one better than this, and had the Director himself jump up to demonstrate how to speak the lines in that over-emphatic way teachers adopt when they are trying to get a point across. (...)

The moment when Mme Pace enters unannounced as the seventh Character afforded another chance to develop the teasing. The Actors no longer stood back stupefied, but in fear rushed wildly off the stage into the auditorium, so by physical association encouraging the audience's own uncertainty. All this suggests that Pirandello was aware, well ahead of his time, that to break out of the proscenium arch was to induce a new level of dramatic experience. (...)

The greatest trick in the *Six Characters* of 1925 was to extend the shock ending. In the revision, Pirandello did not disclose the fate of the two children until the last possible moment. In this way, the drowning of the little Girl and the suicide of the Boy came as a complete surprise, so that their unreality was left far more in question. When the Director called for lights, Pirandello did not allow the curtain to fall. He calculated that at such a moment, when an audience was on the point of returning to its familiar reality, at a moment of total ambivalence, the play had it most in its grip. The theatre was immediately flooded with light as if some supernatural hand had suddenly pulled the switch. No gentle raising of the lights to ease us back into reality, but, still using the element of theatre, a plunge into another reality. The device was repeated when the Director called yet again for the lights to be switched off: the sudden and immediate blackout was shocking and uncanny. (...)

Six Characters was at first criticized because at the end the Characters seemed more real than the Actors, fiction more real than life, and it appeared that chaos reigned.

NOTES

1. This paper was read to the Pirandello Society at the convention of the Modern Language Association of America, San Francisco, December 28, 1979.

2. One thinks of Molière's *L'Impromptu de Versailles* as his Pirandellian play.

5. See Pirandello, *On Humor*, trans. Antonio Illiano and Daniel P. Testa (Chapel Hill, N.C., 1974).

> —J. L. Styan, "Pirandellian Theatre Games: Spectator as Victim," *Modernism in European Drama: Ibsen, Strindberg, Pirandello, Beckett, Essays from Modern Drama*, eds. Frederick J. Marker and Christopher Innes (University of Toronto Press, 1998): 181–90.

PLOT SUMMARY OF

Henry IV

Pirandello wrote *Right You Are (If You Think You Are)* in 1916, *Six Characters in Search of an Author* in 1920, and *Henry IV*, or *Enrico IV*, in 1921. The proximity of the three, particularly the last two, would seem to indicate that he was as concerned with the thematic exploration of madness and its causes as he was with the exploitation of the theatrical possibilities. *Right You Are, Six Characters*, and *Henry IV* all interconnect, as does *Tonight We Improvise*, though written later (1928). A connection between the two motifs may be said to exist in that madness amounts to an attempt to bring painful circumstances into a manageable context; similarly, Pirandello's "theatre" plays attempt to remediate the theatrical traditions that stultify players, plays, and playwrights. In both the madness theme and the theatrical focus, efforts to bring about solutions elicit opposition among those who have not experienced extreme pain and those who have encouraged rigidity and stratified character interpretation. In both cases, the situations are evaluated by the unimaginative who readily dismiss any innovator in thought or action.

In *Henry IV*, the main character's madness results from an accident caused by what we later learn is a malicious spooking of his horse. When he regains consciousness after his fall, he remembers only that he was Henry IV. That is, he becomes the character whom he has been masquerading. The play begins with a scene in which three young men hired for the roles of "counselors" to Henry explain the situation to a fourth character, Berthold, who has just joined the group, thus providing the background. Berthold has made an error that might have happened to the audience without the exposition—this Henry is not the king of France but rather Henry IV of Germany. Berthold is annoyed with his error, for it has cost him some good time studying the wrong period and country. He knows nothing about the German Henry, nor who his own character is, but his new companions also have no idea who their roles are either, except that they are counselors dressed in the period clothing of their originals. Landolph says they are no more than puppets, dressed, ready, but incapable of being anything but form, i.e., actors such as those in *Six Characters*. They promise to help Berthold prepare his role. They also provide an explanation of the two portraits, one of which is Henry in his role as Henry and the other of Matilda as she was when Henry was thrown from his horse. They describe Matilda as Henry's worst enemy, the powerful Marchioness of Tuscany. The counselors would thus seem to have no knowledge of Henry's actual feelings toward Matilda. When John, an ordinary servant, enters to tell them that the Marchioness and her daughter have arrived, they are astonished, but their response includes their opinion that Henry will be displeased with her presence. They order John not to allow Henry to come into the throne room.

Matilda, drawn to her portrait, admires it despite seeing clearly that it now resembles her daughter Frida far more than it does her. Despite her lover Belcredi's rather cruel remarks about the portrait, Matilda, in gazing at it, experiences sensations of her youth again, a transfer to that earlier woman and that earlier time when she was the girl that her daughter now replicates.

The Doctor, to gain some detail of the circumstances, asks Matilda if the portrait was a gift to Henry. She replies that she gave the portrait at the request of Di Nolli's mother, Henry's sister, some four years after his fall. Di Nolli has promised his mother, who has recently died, that he will pull Henry fully back into sanity, for she was convinced sometime before her death that he was very close to being sane again.

The doctor then questions them about the pageant in which Henry took the fall from his horse. Belcredi admits that it was he who caused the accident and tells the story of the pageant in which it emerges that Henry assumed the Henry IV costume and role so that he might be near Matilda. Belcredi in the telling forces Matilda to admit that she did not even like Henry, and seeing the dazed look that possessed him when he saw her, she could not help but laugh. Moreover he frightened her, and not being courageous, she added her derisive laughter to that of the others who made sport of him. She maintains that Henry always loved life more than others, yet at times he grew angry when he "exalted" himself, for he knew that assuming a role that was not his own separated him from his own reality. Belcredi contributes to the description as Matilda presents it, Henry's personality a point on which they agree. He comments finally that Henry was a fine actor. Di Nolli adds that Henry's madness has made his acting superb.

Belcredi is reminded that they all thought Henry was acting when he rejoined them some two hours after the horse and Henry fell. When he reentered the group who were celebrating their pageant, they began to welcome him with hits from their fans and sticks, but he drew his sword and threatened them. The look on his face, now transformed by madness into a horror that frightened them all, was no mask but his new reality. He had become Henry IV, a furious and terrible Henry.

One of his attendants rushes in at this point. The novice Berthold begins to see his fellows as madmen, and he wants to leave immediately. The others come in blaming the new masquer for Henry's fury and his intention to arraign Berthold in the throne room. Now Frida and the Doctor (or so it seems) want to leave. Matilda and Belcredi are willing to see Henry, but costumes must be provided for them. Matilda is to wear the crown of "Duchess Adelaide," mother of the Marchioness (now Frida), and a long cloak that will hide her other clothes. Belcredi is to be a Benedictine monk attending the doctor now disguised as Hugh, Abbot of Cluny.

When Henry emerges, Pirandello describes Henry's eyes as possessing a frightening look that contradicts his penitential sackcloth garment. He bows to Matilda and the Doctor, but eyes Belcredi with suspicion, calling out that he is no monk, but rather Peter Damiani. As if he had gained control of himself, he relents and speaks words of gratitude to Belcredi for having hindered him. In the midst, however, of bowing to Belcredi, he seems to have another thought that incenses him and points an accusing finger at Belcredi, saying that he was the one who started the rumor that Henry's mother had an affair with the Bishop of Augusta.

Henry then focuses on Matilda, saying that if she is there and he is in sackcloth, then he must be only twenty-six years old and his mother is still alive. He mentions his dyed hair, saying that although it is not a reality for the "Duchess Adelaide," it is somewhat for him. But he then considers her purpose in dying her hair—to fool the image in her mirror just a little. Nonetheless, as he would have it, her dyed hair is more serious than his, for his is only a joke. Hers is masquerade. Obviously, Henry has recognized Matilda. He yanks off the sackcloth, throwing it from him, under the guise of rejoicing that on the next day, he will sign the deposition of Gregory VII, and there will be no more Pope. Only a false monk, he exults. This last obviously refers to Belcredi's disguise. Henry retreats then to his sackcloth and previous litany. He grows alternately more and more grandiose and abject, presenting a discourse that concludes with his sweeping magnificently out of the room and Matilda weeping.

As Act II begins, Belcredi and the Doctor speak of Henry's present mental state, but they cannot agree. Donna Matilda has been listening desultorily, but enters their conversation when the Doctor says that Henry's behavior is childish. The Doctor has his learned explanation of Henry's condition, but Donna Matilda understands that Henry is not being childish, but rather is no longer insane. She interprets his speech as directed almost entirely to her. Belcredi objects, insisting that Henry focused on him the whole time. He is quieted, however, by Donna Matilda's asking him if he knows why Henry displayed such animosity toward him and him alone. To her, it is obvious that Henry recognizes also that Belcredi is her lover. The Doctor accepts none of this, returning instead to his analysis, convinced that the trick they have planned—to dress Frida in Matilda's pageant attire—will bring Henry to sanity. Frida arrives and is indeed the image of her mother's portrait.

As they are about to pretend to go away, one of Henry's attendants comes to ask if they will go in to Henry in their costumes, telling him that the Marchioness of Tuscany has gotten the Pope to agree to see Henry. Henry has expressed the fear that the Marchioness has been displeased with his love for her and will turn the Pope further against him. Not only does Donna Matilda believe she understands Henry's meaning in the message he has sent out, but by now Belcredi accepts that Henry wishes to know whether she welcomes his love for her. Thus Belcredi answers sardonically for her that she no longer has an aversion to Henry. She corrects his statement by saying that she intends to show Henry that contrary to what he supposed, her feelings were warm toward him at the time of the Pageant.

Henry's attendant suggests that she then wear the gown of the Marchioness, but the Doctor objects. His present plan will work no better than his others since Henry is no longer mad. Throughout Pirandello presents the Doctor as ineffectual; Belcredi states that he cannot imagine why the Doctor or alienist, as psychologists were then called, did not go to law school rather than medical school since all he does is talk.

Henry speaks of Donna Matilda's daughter, but he obscures his intent. Although his discourse aims at the daughter being his wife, Donna Matilda accepts that he speaks only to her of his love and she responds positively. He grows excited, then abruptly sends them away. When they leave, however, he reveals his sanity to his attendants. Interestingly, he trusts them. He does not trust Matilda, however, and certainly not Belcredi.

The crude devise that the Doctor has planned for Henry is to replace the portraits of Henry and Matilda with Frida in the costume of the Marchioness of Tuscany and Henry's nephew in the garb of Henry IV within the frames. Act III opens with them in place. Henry enters, walking slowly to his apartment. Frida whispers his name. He is filled with terror, thinking that he has gone mad again. She whispers again. He drops the lamp he carries, moving as if to run; she jumps down from the frame, screaming in terror. Di Nolli jumps down and goes to her; the others come running in. They have by now been told by Henry's attendants that he is no longer insane, and has been acting for some time. Belcredi would have it that Henry has been deceiving all of them—all who have acted in "good faith"—playing a joke on them, which gives no cognizance to the suffering that Henry has endured for the twenty years.

Belcredi alone has something to fear from Henry's sanity, however. Henry responds by giving a summary of the slow pace of his madness and the impossibility of reentering the society he knew after the harrowing experience of the twenty years he has been shut away. He reminds Belcredi that it was he who always furiously insisted that Henry was mad before the fall. Belcredi insists that he was merely joking. Henry cannot accept any of it as joking and says that to reenter is comparable to arriving at a banquet that is not only finished but also no evidence of its occurrence remains. Henry then speaks of the injury to his horse, pricking of his horse until it bled as Belcredi rode behind him, causing it to bolt and Henry to fall.

When he found himself sane after so long, he preferred to remain mad, living his consciousness in a fantasy in the world that he created, apart from the one who occasioned the madness and the others who have come to create a mad and dangerous fantasy in the notion that they could cure the tragedy of his life.

Henry embraces Frida, for it is she who images the dream that Belcredi destroyed for him, not the aged Matilda. Belcredi would attack Henry to free Frida, but Henry kills him with Landolph's sword. Belcredi's last words are that Henry's "not mad." But this will never be believed, and Henry and his attendants are once more united, this time forever.

LIST OF CHARACTERS IN

Henry IV

Henry IV fell off his horse after it was spooked by Belcredi in a Pageant. He was costumed as Henry IV when the accident occurred and awoke believing that he was Henry IV. His trauma rendered him insane for twelve years, but when the play begins, he has been sequestered in his palatial surroundings for twenty years. He knows that he is no longer insane, but no one else knows it.

Marchioness Matilda Spina is the woman with whom Henry was in love at the time of his fall. Although she was not indifferent to him, she found most things humorous, including men's love for her.

Frida, the Marchioness' daughter, ordinarily merely resembles her mother, but when she puts on the Gown worn in the Pageant, she becomes the very image of her mother at her age. She is to be married to Henry's nephew Charles Di Nolli.

Charles Di Nolli has promised his mother, the sister of Henry, that he will try to bring Henry back to sanity. She has the sense that Henry has regained his sanity or very nearly so.

Baron Tito Belcredi was the perpetrator of Henry's accident. He is now Matilda's lover, though they do not seem especially fond of each other.

Doctor Dionysius Genoni is a psychiatrist, but he is presented as only a man of words, words, words—none of which could be efficacious for anyone. His ineptitude creates more difficulties than it solves.

CRITICAL VIEWS ON

Henry IV

HASKELL M. BLOCK ON PIRANDELLO'S TRANSFORMATION OF TRADITIONAL THEATER

[Professor of Comparative Literature at Brooklyn College of the City University of New York, Haskell M. Block also wrote *Mallarme and the Symbolist Drama*.]

Those who contend that tragedy is dead commonly have in mind tragic drama as written by the Greeks or the Elizabethans, or tragedy as defined by Aristotle. There can be no doubt that the concept of tragedy has undergone considerable change in our time, to the point where commentators speak of a "tragic vision" or a "tragic sense of life" that is wholly independent of theatrical performance. Yet, for most readers and spectators, tragedy continues to be viewed essentially as a dramatic form, and in the drama of the twentieth century, mixed forms dominate the scene. The characteristic serious play in modern drama is likely to be tragicomedy or grotesque farce. This does not mean, however, that the concept of tragedy has disappeared; rather, that it has been transformed.

The arguments against the possibility of tragedy in our time are too well known to warrant detailed recapitulation. Realism, determinism, the decline of myth, a diminished view of man, the absence of community between playwright and audience—these are among the most common explanations. They serve, it seems to me, only to explain why tragedy in strict conformity to a classical model is impossible; but rather than speak of the death of tragedy, we would do better to consider its persistence through transformation. (...)

By way of brief illustration, we may single out the character of the tragic hero. The older protagonists were necessarily highborn and powerful, persons on whom the fate of communities depended. Yet, the monumentality of an Oedipus or a Hamlet is not only an expression of his political and social role. It is derived from the depth, intensity, and complexity of his suffering, a suffering through which the tragic hero acquires a knowledge of himself and of the human condition that he and we could not have gained in any other way. (...)

I should like to argue that this same nobility and grandeur may be found in the modern tragic theatre. This contention is not new. It was forcefully asserted by Schiller in his view of sublime emotion as the end of tragedy; the beauty of tragedy, he insists, is in the exaltation of the hero over his suffering. His natural greatness is present as an affirmation of nobility of character transcending any physical suffering. (...)

The paradoxical ennoblement of the tragic hero follows from his illumination, from the new knowledge gained of himself and the world as a result of his trial. (...)

[T]he modern repertoire includes plays in which the suffering and self-knowledge central to the tragic hero are unmistakably present, even though the interiorization of experience and the psychological preoccupations of modern drama have made for new conceptions of both characterization and action. (...)

Pirandello's *Enrico IV* is altogether representative of the interiorization of tragedy in modern times. A brief analysis might help to show the accord of Pirandello's tragic hero and traditional conceptions in both drama and criticism.

It is at least of interest to note that Pirandello subtitled *Enrico IV*, "tragedia in tre atti." His hero is an emperor only in fantasy, but that fantasy is far more real and more durable than ordinary everyday experience. It is enough for the well-to-do Italian gentleman who imagines himself to be an emperor to claim the role in order to raise himself to the plane of exceptionality. His role, however, is far more an expression of inner rather than external power. There is nothing mean or sordid about his character, a fitting reminder that in modern drama tragic nobility is not a matter of class or wealth. Enrico IV bears his greatness within himself and expresses it both in his acts and in his realizations. The drama of suffering and ennoblement lies essentially within.

Pirandello's play, like all of his major plays, depends for its dramatic movement on the interaction of mask and reality, on a view of life as masquerade asserting itself in lavish theatricality of costume and gesture. The stage directions tell us of Enrico's "tragico pallore," but the intensity of his suffering can be gauged only when the play is read or seen retrospectively. For the hero's masquerade at the outset is an act of conscious volition. Pirandello blurs the lines between "sanity" and "madness," just as he questions the ability of words to render intense personal experience. Enrico lives his fantasy with passion and even, at times, with fury; our subsequent discovery of his lucidity does not make him any the less exceptional. His way of seeing and living is not like that of anyone else. (...)

[W]hy did Pirandello consider his play to be a tragedy? (...)

[T]he tragedy lies within the hero, in his "madness" from a willed and lucid choice to a coercive and inescapable necessity. The permanent loss of freedom is recognized in Enrico's last line: "ora si ... per forza ... qua insieme, qua insieme ... e per sempre!" Enrico is thus his own victim, imprisoned in his mask. His suffering is the loss of his essential freedom, even though he transcends this suffering in his-realization of his imprisonment. (...)

Pirandello is among the few modern playwrights who have been able to invest a hero with tragic grandeur. Needless to say, this hero is not in any way average or typical or representative. His exceptionality lies not in any ability to perform deeds, but in his rare insight into the human condition and his recognition of the consequences of his choices. It is this insight and honesty which endow the hero's knowledge with dignity and universality.

—Haskell M. Block, "Some Notes on the Problem of Modern Tragedy," *Comparative Literature Studies*, 9:1 (University of Illinois Press, 1972): 80–84.

[A renowned theater critic, translator, playwright, and considered to be Pirandello's canonical critic, Eric Bentley has written extensively on the theater. In this extract Bentley discusses the play's historical roots]

The question with a work of art that is notably obscure is whether the first puzzling acquaintance one had with it afforded such a premium of pleasure that one wishes to come back for more. In the case of *Enrico IV* there can surely be little doubt. At first encounter, it is hard to get the facts straight-and therefore impossible to get the meaning straight-but there is no doubt of the powerful impression made by the principle images, speeches, and scenes. The general scheme is itself very striking for anyone with the slightest predilection for Gothic fiction, and there are moments of exquisite theatrical poetry-such as the moment in which Henry dictates his life story to Giovanni-which make their mark even before we ask questions about the main drift.

When we do come to these questions, the first question of all is inevitably: what about this German Emperor? Why did it have to be him? I thought I might find some clues when I found mentioned by Benjamin Cremieux the titles of the books Pirandello had consulted on the subject: Voight's life of Pope Gregory VII and Oncken's *Allgemeine Geschichte*. But I did not find much in these that seemed more to the purpose than an encyclopedia article on the subject unless it was two pictures-of the Abbey of Cluny and the palace at Goslar, respectively. Pirandello worked with the elementary facts of Henry's life as they might be related by any history teacher. Because Henry came to the throne as a mere child, his mother, Agnes, acted as Regent. She came under suspicion of adultery with the Bishop of Augsburg and had to be removed. To this bit of pure history Pirandello adds the fiction that the accusation of adultery was brought about by an ecclesiastical friend of the Vatican's: Peter Damiani. Aside from this, all that is filled in of Henry's earlier life is that he had trouble keeping his German barons and ecclesiastics in line. Pirandello, like other people, is mainly interested in what happened when Henry was twenty-six; namely, his arch-enemy, the Pope, brought him literally to his knees and he knelt in the snow hoping that the Pope would give him an audience. His wife, the Empress Bertha, knelt with him, and Bertha's mother Duchess Adelaide, went with the Abbot of Cluny, another friendly witness, to plead with the Pope and the latter's ally, Countess Matilda of Tuscany.

Here Pirandello adds something of more significance than the involvement of Peter Damiani. "I wanted," he has been quoted as saying, "a situation where a historical personage was in love with a woman who was his enemy." Not finding what he wanted, he created it. Matilda of Tuscany was indeed Henry IV's enemy, but no historical records that he loved her. Pirandello invents this motif, and lets us know it in the play itself by having Landolf remark that Henry secretly loves Matilda even though the historians say nothing about it. It is only through his own Matilda that Pirandello's nameless young protagonist comes to the Emperor Henry IV in the first place. The modern Matilda had already picked her medieval namesake as her role in the masquerade, and that is what gave her young man the idea of being Henry:

> I said I'd like to be Countess Matilda of Tuscany.... I just heard him saying, "Then I'll be at your feet in Canossa...." I now understood why he wanted to be next to me in the cavalcade as the Emperor ... because I'd chosen to represent his implacable enemy.

And because he secretly loved her. What the nameless young man finds in history besides a name and the status of emperor is a relationship of love-hate.

Pirandello's Emperor seems most of the time stuck in his twenty-sixth year (1077), but he has some power to bob about in his private time machine, and is particularly concerned with the years 1076 and 1080. In 1076 at Tribur the German princes had proposed to depose Henry. His famous gesture at Canossa turns out on further scrutiny not to be a sincere and definitive submission before Papal authority but a sly man's effort to head off the prospect of facing his accusers. By 1080 Henry's position

had been strengthened to the point where it was not *his* throne
that was in danger but the Pope's own. This was an emperor who,
when the Pope was not to his liking, would set up another: the
Henry of Pirandello's play prophesies that at Brixen he will
declare Pope Gregory deposed. That the historical Emperor
outlived by many years both Canossa and Brixen is
acknowledged by Pirandello only in the statement that his life
contained the material for many tragedies.

It would be a mistake to pursue the historical Henry past the
point where Pirandello takes leave of him, or to hunt for more
parallels than the play immediately suggests to anyone who
knows the historical outline, for beyond this point history will
become the play's rival and a victorious rival at that. By putting
into the play itself the few historical facts he needs, the author is
declaring the other facts off limits. After all, drawing upon some
very suggestive incidents and relationships, he has created a plot
and characters that are his own and not at all medieval. We
perhaps need to brush aside the Gothic trappings altogether for
a minute or two if we are to glimpse his characters as they are.

—Eric Bentley, "*Enrico IV*: The Tragic Emperor," *Tulane Drama Review* 10, 3 (Spring 1966).

SUSAN BASSNETT ON *HENRY IV* AS TRAGEDY

[Susan Bassnett, Professor in the Comparative
Literature Department at the University of Warwick in
England, has written on Sylvia Plath, Elizabeth I, and
Bernhardt, Terry, and Duse, in addition to Pirandello.]

Approaching the theater of Pirandello, it becomes immediately
obvious that there are no easy labels to attach to this work. Some
of his plays, notably the theater-in-the-theater trilogy, show his
ability to experiment with theater form, while others conform to
the well-made three-act play of the naturalist theater tradition
but deal with the theme of multiplicity in human relationships
and the tragedy of man's search for a universally recognized
identity. Time and again Pirandello explores themes that were to
recur later in the century in the theater of the absurd and the
theater of cruelty. The fact that it is impossible to label

Pirandello clearly is a nicely ironic touch that he would himself have liked, for in all his work he was concerned primarily with the idea of the impossibility of truth. Again and again his writings illustrate the idea of relativity, of a many-sidedness that denies the existence of a single absolute. Even language, the instrument of man's daily communication, is inadequate. As the Father says in *Six Characters in Search of an Author*:

> Don't you see that the whole trouble lies here? In words. Each of us has within him a whole world of things, each one has his own special world. And how can we ever come to an understanding if I put into the words I utter the sense and value of things as I see them.

Nor is identity a unique fact. In *Right You Are (If You Think So)* Signora Ponza, the mystery lady that the Neighbors in the play seek to explain, refuses any single definition of her relationship to the man claiming to be her husband and the woman claiming to be her mother and says simply, "I am whoever you believe me to be." Pirandello acknowledges the impossibility of single definitions or simple solutions and offers us a vision of the world in which nothing is ever certain. (...)

Considerable attention has been given to Pirandello's experiments with theater form. Indeed, his reputation is largely that of an innovative dramatist, but of all his plays the one that stands out in terms of emphasis on a single character is *Henry IV*. This is the most frequently performed play by Pirandello in English, and has frequently been compared to *Hamlet*. (...)

The relativity of madness is the pivotal point of the whole play and from this various other aspects of relativity are touched on. In this respect, *Henry IV* provides almost a resume of the principal themes of Pirandello's theater—the relativity of perception and of language, the relativity of freedom, existence seen as imprisonment in itself, the notion of life as a game wherein each person plays an assigned role. The first scene of the play, which serves as a comic vehicle to provide the audience with details of Henry's situation, immediately introduces some of these themes. When Bertoldo discovers that he has read up on the wrong time period, like an actor learning the wrong part, he asks the others who he is supposed to be in the eleventh-century court where they play their roles. Landolfo replies: "And you can comfort yourself with the fact that we don't know who we are either. He's Arialdo; he's Ordulfo; I'm Landolfo ... That's what he calls us. We're used to it now. But who are we? Names of that time period." The retainers exist only as names and have no place in history, no part other than what Henry determines they will play. They exist because of Henry and for him; he alone has a notion of who they are, because, as Landolfo says, he has at least labeled them with names. In assuming these roles, they have sacrificed not only any identity they may have had in the twentieth century, but because they do not believe in what they are doing, they also treat the whole thing as a joke and do not even live as people in the eleventh century. Just as the Spectators in *Each in His Own Way* were characterized and named by their opinions, so these retainers have lost everything except the names given to them by a man they believe is mad.

Landolfo explains further that they are puppets, to be manipulated by Henry:

> We're like this, without anyone to give us a clue or give us a scene to play. How shall I put it? The form is there, but without any content. We're worse off than the real privy counsellors of Henry IV because, true, no one gave them a part to play either, but at least they didn't know they were supposed to be playing one. They played a part because they played it. Only it wasn't a part, it was their life.

This speech takes us back to *Questa sera si recita*, where the actors claim that they must live their roles or be nothing. The four retainers, superficially comic though they appear to be, are trapped in an even more tragic situation than Henry or Giovanni who play their roles with a kind of conviction. The retainers' role-playing is without direction or purpose, and they are entirely at the whim of a madman. If we extend this situation onto a more universal level, the retainers can be seen as a man and the madman in control is chance, or god. (...)

If life is inconstancy and motion, as Pirandello reiterates in play after play, and man is constantly striving to create a niche for himself beyond that movement, then the madman, unaware of his "privilege," is the one with the insight into what being alive means. In a universe of motion, the madness is to strive for fixity, not to live out a life of formless movement. In *On Humor* Pirandello tells us that:

> The collective consciousness, the soul of the race of which we are a part lives within each of us; and the ways in which others judge and feel and act pressure us subconsciously. In society, masks, disguises and pretence control operations—the more habitual they become, the less we are aware of them; and in the same way, we mask our real self, pretending to be other than we are, adopting a dual, even a manifold "persona".

In such a context, the "sane" man is the more mad since he lives out a daily delusion that constancy is possible. The irony of the play is in the realizations: those declared by some to be "mad" because they do not conform to the social norms are less "mad" than those who believe in the existence of absolutes, but whatever their state of madness or sanity, all men are condemned to exist in a world of motion and time, from which even illusion is no valid escape. Moreover, since illusion is itself formless, man seeks stability through an indefinable abstract, the ultimate absurdity. (...)

Henry is supposedly mad in Act I, declares himself sane in Act II, commits a "mad" gesture in Act III, where, it must be noted, the stage directions are deliberately ambiguous, and Henry is described as laughing like a madman. But Henry is consistent in his real or feigned madness. The truths he speaks in Act I when we all believe he is mad are reiterated in Act II when he "proves" his sanity by admitting that he knows he is playing a role and living in another time period. He changes moods abruptly, moves about in time, and physically he moves rapidly round the stage, going from person to person in Act I. In Acts II and III he moves in and out of apparent sanity; his moods seem more controlled, his movements are less pronounced, but his cynicism and sufferings are constantly present.

As the play progresses, it becomes increasingly clear that we are being shown that language, perception, and finally reality are all relative, and that the great problem facing man is how to communicate with his fellows. Henry, the madman, must follow up his words with actions to prove their "truth" to the others, so he has to show the four retainers how he can act and construct scenes before they believe he is "cured," and in the final act he communicates by committing a violent action, murder, which ironically "proves" to the others only that their beliefs are confirmed and he is mad after all. His final gesture, the murder of Belcredi, is inevitable because on one level it is his last desperate attempt to show that his role is real and not a game and cannot be dismissed as easily as the others presume, and on another level it is the action of a man trapped into a comer and forced to react. (...)

The Visitors are real, their attempts to "cure" him do happen, and he can no longer insist on closing himself in the eleventh century to escape. At the conclusion of the play, the realization of how this reality has trapped him forever forcibly in a role he previously played of his own free will is emphasized by the stage directions, and by Henry's words:

> Yes, now ... inevitably ... (gathers his retainers round him, as if to shield himself,) here together, here together ... forever! (...)

Henry is finally condemned to being the mad Emperor because he tried to play a role and create an illusion to save himself pain. No one can escape in the end, and the fake world of recreated history is as inadequate as the makeup Matilda wears to disguise her age.

The disguise motif, so crucial to the play, moves from being comic in the first scene to the tragic moments at the end of the play, when Henry realizes that he will never be able to take off his costume.

—Susan Bassnett, "Henry IV—The Tragic Humorist," *A Companion to Pirandello Studies* (Greenwood Press, 1991): 231–33.

Luisetta Chomel on Futility of Transcending Time

[Luisetta Chomel is Professor of Modern and Classical Languages at the University of Houston. She has published *D'Annunzio: un teatro al femminile* (Longo, 1997).]

The Pirandellian man, trapped in the flux of time, condemned to endure an incessant chain of transformations, vainly tries to resist time and fix himself in a lasting form. Institutions, traditions, social masks, even prejudices and hypocrisy are but devices he uses in his attempt to stop the flow of time. The time motif punctuates Pirandello's writings from the poetic beginning to the last plays, in different forms and various degrees of intensity. (...)

The past remains a shadowy zone of life, a construction of the mind rather than a reality. In "La signora Frola e il signor Ponza", the past of the newly arrived trio, anxiously sought by the little community of the town, has practically disappeared with the documents destroyed by the earthquake. What remains of it are the opposite versions given by Signora Frola and Signor Ponza. Where is the truth? Or what is the past? The past is not what really happened but how the individual, now, perceives it. Only the present has an indisputable value while previous events vanish in the imponderable night of subjective consciousness. Reciprocal compassion for the common folly appears to be the single attainable goal of human experience. (...)

Chronological time is, for Pirandello, the beating heart of life; a senseless life, in its self-destroying sequence of unrelated events; but still life, beyond which there is only madness or death. Only the forms of art are spared by the erosion of time, but life is not art. In *Sei personaggi in cerca di autore*, the six individuals who burst upon the stage during the rehearsal, present themselves as living creatures, striving to transcend their particular nature and become universal characters in a play.

When the Director addressing the Father asks: "E lei, con codesti signori attorno è nato personaggio?", the answer is "Appunto signore. E vivi come ci vede." The six characters are personifications of the "informe vita che anela alla sua forma", and their attempt symbolizes man's aspiration to transcend temporal relativity and enter the absolute reality of timeless forms, created by art. Their drama will not be transformed into a form of art, and the six characters fall back into their shapeless lives. Their deception reflects life's attempt to attain an atemporal dimension.[10]

Enrico IV presents the same drama but viewed from the other side since to withdraw from time is the equivalent of non-living. Fixed in the absolute past of his historical role, Enrico lives in a timeless dimension, where present and future are both denied. When, awakening from his folly, he chooses to remain in his retreat, the decision is dictated by his awareness that life is in time. For twelve years madness has kept him in a perennial youth, an unchanging sphere of nonlife, while the others were living, loving, suffering and changing. Like for Mattia Pascal, there is no room left for him at the banquet of life. But, unlike Mattia, he refuses to resume his name. His previous existence, amputated of twelve years of time, looks crippled, unworthy to be lived. Days and years flow in an eventless, preordered sequence, when life surreptitiously creeps into his secluded villa. The presence of Matilde and Belcredi stirs old passions of love and rivalry, and suddenly life burst forth, crashing with its impetus the carefully preserved form of the past. The present affirms itself. Henry is back in time asserting his right to live, to love and avenge. The tragedy, suspended for many years, explodes, and he kills his rival. After the crime, when he has no other escape but his old imposture, the retreat into timelessness appears in his anguishing reality as a tomb in which he buries himself: "Ora si ... per forza ... qua insieme ... e per sempre."[11]

If *Sei personaggi in cerca autore* and *Enrico IV* illustrate the futility of human attempts to transcend time, *Come tu mi vuoi* addresses the problem at its core, showing the inevitable dissolution of interior personality when considered in the only perspective of chronological time. Memory is the only bridge between past and present, but even this faculty is unreliable. Past happenings, recalled by different persons and distorted by individual interpretations, lose their compact reality and dissolve in contradictory opinions. What has been is as uncertain as what will be.

NOTES

10. In *Enrico IV* Pirandello, reversing the typical formula of popular "Piradellianism", has reached a conclusion diametrically opposite to it. This thesis is supported by Eric Bentley in his critical essay on *Enrico IV*. "His hero tried to go on being the twenty-six-years-old German Emperor, yet he not only could not build himself a heaven in fantasy, but longed for the other life, the twentieth-century one, that he was missing" (p. 53).

11. Pirandello's last plays represent a drastic departure from the dialectic of his previous theater. This further development of his artistic creation, which has not found a unanimous approval among the critics, can be viewed as the ultimate attempt made by the writer to overcome his tragic vision of life. Pirandello felt compelled to renew himself under the impulse of the surrealistic movement which was spreading in Europe at that time. A note left by Pirandello himself seems to sustain this hypothesis. "Anche perchè l'autore famoso non riesce più a vedersi naturalmente, ma secondo la luce in cui lo ha messo la fama, alla quale bisogna che egli si adatti sforzando la propria natura. Un'altra ragione è poi determinata dal sapere l'autore che la sua nuova opera è attesa, e questo fa sì che egli non lasci libertà d'azione alla propria natura, ma presieda con la riflessione al proprio lavoro." *Saggi, poesie, scritti varii*, p. 1211. "Libertà d'azione" for Pirandello means passion. Reflexion by itself cannot convey the full participation in the human drama that is the characteristic of Pirandello's writings.

—Luisetta Chomel, "Pirandello's Notion of Time," *Canadian Journal of Italian Studies* 12 (1989): 26–39.

ALBERTO DE VIVO ON HENRY'S TIME PERCEPTION

[Alberto De Vivo published his essay *"Henry IV* and Time," in the *Canadian Journal of Italian Studies* (1989).]

Historically, time has been viewed in two opposed ways.[1] Some theories like indeterminism and relativism, describe it as an "epistemological uncertainty."[2] Other theories, like determinism and absolutism,[3] describe it as an epistemological certainty. For indeterminists time is flux, movement, change, difference, openness—in this paper I will refer to this time simply by the term *time*. For determinists, it is fixed, always the same, closed, and, as for Newton,[4] absolute. In the context of Pirandello's *Henry IV*, deterministic time will refer to all those activities—emotional, physical or mental—that stop the flux of time, that spatialize it, that transform time into Newtonian space—a term that I will often use in order to refer to deterministic time. (...)

What is Henry's view of time? How does he feel about it? In order to answer this question, it is necessary to identify, first, Henry's era. Is it the eleventh century, the beginning of the twentieth century, or the 1920's? Clearly the 1071 of the historical emperor Henry IV is not the time of Pirandello's Henry, nor is this time the main focus of the thoughts about time of Pirandello's characters. Henry's place in chronological time must be either 1900 or 1920, or both.

These three chronological eras function as indices of the temporal framework of the text. They tell us that the story's time consists of three historical periods. The year 1922 represents the present reflected, in the story, by the visit by Matilde, Frida, Belcredi and Dr. Di Nolli, and its consequences for Henry. The year 1900 represents the actual beginning of the story—when Henry was about twenty six and in love with Matilde, when the cavalcade in costume took place and Henry fell, becoming mad and believing himself to be Henry IV. The year 1071 refers to the crucial event in the life of Emperor Henry when he was penitent at Canossa which Pirandello's Henry uses in a strategic way in order to deconstruct the deterministic tendencies of time. (...)

Clearly life-time is seen by Henry as movement, change, difference, as indeterminate, full of "incognite," made up of events that are not explainable and therefore should be cause of wonder. Yet it is this kind of events which are suppressed by those who believe themselves to be what they are not and thus keep on living as if they had never taken place. Such a character is Belcredi, for whom, without any wonder or marvel, "life tomorrow will be exactly like today" (326). For him, as for the other aristocrats, nothing ever changes, time is forever repetition, sameness, space, determinism. Unlike Belcredi, Henry perceives as a "condemnation" (328), which he can no longer bear, the transformation of his own time into space—reflected by his fixed mask of the King Henry IV at the age of twenty-six, as in the painting. So he asks his visitors to "implore" the pope to free him from his chain of absolute time in order to live again that life from which he has been excluded.

This lyrical appeal of time as living flux is so profound, so touching and sincere, that we cannot but ask: why did he not return to the living life when he regained consciousness? We will not answer this crucial question now, but we will try later.

In Henry's second dialogue, in the second act, we learn how he feels about his historical time and his society, about life in the early twenties. (...)

Henry knows that, in reality, we all interpret words differently, that we are not alike, that we are not what others think we are, not even the way we think we are, since each of us is one and many at the same time. He knows that selfhood, like the living present, is a network of possibilities; that indeterminism, subjective relativism, is the ground of experience and of the experiencer. Nevertheless he is also painfully aware of the fact that this form of time is not the ground of social life since people, almost naturally, displace it by transforming it into a dogmatic determinism.

Henry's critique of these spatializing activities illustrates his position on both time and space. (...)

Yet soon after—when he tells us that we do not have the power to spatialize our own temporality and that of others, that we do not have the freedom to determine the events of the day, our own destiny or history, because we are ourselves determined by the past—it is a different image of time that he proposes: no longer open but closed. Traditions, customs and language determine what we say, what we do, and what we are so there is no originality, freedom, openness. Time now seems forever fixed, forever spatialized. (...)

If this were Henry's last word on the matter it would leave us with an unsolvable paradox since we would not know which conception represents Pirandello's philosophy of time: the one which sees time as open or the one which sees it as closed. Of course, this is not the case. In fact, soon after, still in the second act—when he speaks about the logic of the madman counter posing it to that of the non-mad—he criticizes the logic of the latter for its foundationalist, constructivist character since it is the tool which the non-mad people use to create the fixed images that they superimpose on themselves and others—the tool used by Matilde to mask herself as a younger woman and by Belcredi to label Henry as a madman. He describes such constructions as illusions, but as illusions which in our society have the power to create realities and thus to become themselves fixed and stable realities. Unlike the logic of so-called sane people, the logic of mad people is actually illogical, irrational, "inconstant," "as light as a feather," "today like this and tomorrow who knows how!" (352). (...)

Henry makes an important distinction between those who put on a mask "for laughing," like himself, and those who, like Matilde and Belcredi, do it "seriously" (326). Moreover he also draws a distinction between those who are "conscious" and those who are "unconscious" of their mask. He says: "I am cured, gentlemen, because I know perfectly well I am acting mad, here; and I do it quietly!—The trouble is that you live your madness agitatedly, without knowing it and without seeing it" (368). (...)

At this point the question whether Henry really desires to free himself from his mask, as he indicated at the end of his first dialogue, is yes. Ideally, he would like to escape determinism, but, as we have just said, he knows that it is impossible. Consequently he chooses the next best thing: he "consciously" and freely selects to wear a mask, a determined time, but one which allows him at least the freedom to play the game of determinism, transforming it into a comedy. This decision is based on his knowledge that, even if he were to abandon his mask, people would not allow him to live life as it really is: flux, movement, change. Because they would automatically close it by labeling him, judging him, fixing him in the eternal image of a madman and ridicule him as they had before. Given this inevitable outcome, Henry's choice appears most logical.

Moreover, only from within this distanced, fixed time can he obtain the freedom to transform determinism into a comic play which amuses him, allowing him to laugh at his own and everyone else's mask. (...)

[A]s a consequence of killing his arch enemy Belcredi, the personification of determinism itself, Henry does no longer have the choice to play the game of determinism. From now on his mask will be required out of necessity. In order to avoid the consequences of his action he "must" act mad, must make believe he is Henry IV. In this sense the mask is now imposed on him by outside forces, by other social norms. So, while for the previous ten years determinism was a choice which allowed him to play and laugh, from now on determinism is seen as a prison, since it really condemns him to live out the rest of his life as a mad man. Thus, the play *Henry IV* which till now was on the verge of farce, only in the end becomes a tragedy.

NOTES

1. This dualistic conception of time has been clearly expressed by William Barrett in the following manner: "The discussions of time among modern philosophers have tended to become polarized around two radically different kinds of temporality. The distinction has been expressed variously as that between clock time and real duration (Bergson); between actual becoming as the radically discontinuous emergence of events and the continuum of time as mere mathematical possibility (Whitehead); between primordial temporality and the 'vulgar' understanding of time (Heidegger). There is also the common distinction between cosmic and human time; or, in its most crude formulation, between psychological and physical time" ("The Flow of Time" 355).

2. In his essay, "An uncertain Semiotic," Floyd Merrel uses this definition to describe some of the most important theories, in the sciences and in the arts, developed in the twentieth century. Specifically, he uses the term when he discusses Relativity, Quantum Theory, New Cybernetics, and Pierce's Semiotics on pages 251 and 252.

3. After Descartes, Kant is the most important advocate of this view since, according to him, time "is the formal condition a priori of all phenomena whatsoever" (*Critique* 31).

4. In a famous passage, Newton distinguishes real from apparent time, but for him real time is "absolute, true, and mathematical, [and] of itself, and from its own nature, flows equally without relating to anything external" (*The Mathematical Principles*, 16). As such it has nothing to do with living time.

—Alberto De Vivo, "Henry IV and Time," *Canadian Journal of Italian Studies* 12 (1989): 40–50.

[In addition to her work on Pirandello, Maggie Günsberg has written extensively on Italian theatrical history, including work by Machiavelli, Ariosto, Goldoni, and D'Annunzio.]

There are various indications in Pirandello's plays of hysteria as a key component in the construction of a number of his female characters. Whilst relatively minor forms of nervous, emotional disturbance, such as weeping, growing pale and momentary convulsiveness, are mostly, but by no means exclusively, displayed by female characters, symptoms of full hysterical behaviour, by contrast, are confined to the women. Hysteria is firstly, then, to be distinguished from less severe manifestations of nervous disturbance. It is, furthermore, to be regarded as distinct from the generic category of madness, the portrayal of which is also found in the plays, and of which it is definable as a specific type. (...)

In the context of considerations both of gender and social status, it will be argued that certain definitive features of hysteria are exhibited only by female characters, whose social status, moreover, is, mostly, that of 'fallen women' of one type or another. By contrast, as far as the portrayal of cases of madness is concerned, male characters appear to predominate. (...)

As a rejection of socialization, the form of converted response represented by hysteria is clearly not restricted to women, and we shall in fact be examining one male character whose symptoms approximate interestingly to certain aspects of this condition. It has been observed that the Great War produced numerous and varied cases of hysteria in soldiers of all ranks as the excessive demands of a patriarchal ethos of masculinity taken to extremes began to take its toll. Even then, however, the orthodox view was that sufferers were simply reacting in an unmanly fashion; in other words, that they were guilty of exhibiting behaviour associated with femininity [Showalter, 1987, p. 171]. Hysteria was categorized as a variant of the discourse of the body, a discourse in itself assumed to be exclusively and archetypally feminine. (...)

The presence of female characters suffering from nervous disturbance in Pirandello's plays may be attributed at least in part to another well-known biographical fact, namely the prolonged nervous disorder exhibited by his wife. The real causes of Antonietta's symptoms have sadly, and typically, been eclipsed by attention to the more accessible, and culturally more acceptable, symptoms themselves. It is, however, certain that in 1918 she was tricked into entering a 'clinica neurologica', or 'casa di cura' [Giudice, 1963, p. 300]. Here she either found peace until her death thirty years later, or became so institutionalized as to be unable to leave. At any rate, 1924 saw Pirandello's final attempts to take her home, attempts which appear to have begun immediately after her confinement. It is tempting to speculate that his renunciation of Antonietta, and his first encounter with Marta Abba, both of which occurred in 1924, contributed to the more covert nature of the representation of hysteria after that year. In other words, plays after 1924 may well reflect the fact that the writer was less preoccupied with female hysteria than in preceding years. (...)

A closer look at the various received connotations of hysteria which were endemic during Pirandello's era, and which are discernible in his writing, reveals the assumed synonymity of hysteria with madness, with woman/the feminine, and even with feminism. These synonyms interlink in that woman/the feminine has always been essentially associated with madness, or unreason [Lloyd, 1971; Lloyd, 1984; Maclean, 1985]. Feminism was regarded as a form of hysteria in that, as an expression of unreasonable aspirations, it could result in nervous disorder [see Showalter, 1987, ch. 6]. Furthermore, feminists were stereotyped not only in terms of their unreasonableness, but also by their manner and appearance, in such a way as to suggest nervous imbalance. Regarded as denying their femininity by wanting to enter a man's world, they were accused of trying to be masculine, and, in conjunction with this, of not taking the requisite care to appear tidy, well-groomed and feminine. The actual link between hysteria and feminism, both of which are reactions to patriarchal restraints, is that one, namely hysteria, is the impotent underside of its politicized and active other, namely feminism. This association, however, was suppressed by mainstream opinion. (...)

The sheer theatricality of hysteria is self-evident, not only in the physically dramatic nature of many of its symptoms, but also in the equally extreme manner with which the 'remedy' is sometimes administered, as in the case we have just observed. The processes of hysteria therefore provide highly effective stage material. (...)

Central to this drama is the exhibition of the female body itself, of female sexuality both in rebellion and on display. A particularly important aspect of hysteria in female patients is the powerful sexual element which accompanies the dramatic exhibition of a female body in disorder, partly exposed, in convulsions, and out of control.

The resulting manifestly sexualized dynamic of exhibitionism/voyeurism is set up in the case of several of Pirandello's hysterical women, whose portrayal clearly reflects dominant cultural perceptions. One such stereotype, namely the association of loose, dishevelled hair with unbridled, 'immoral' female sexuality/desire, goes back at least as far as the Bible, with the episode of Mary Magdalene, the reformed courtesan traditionally identified as the woman whom Christ allows to dry and anoint his feet with her long hair [Hall, 1974, p. 202]. Untidy hair and disordered clothing which reveals breasts and legs also connote post-coital disarray, and together constitute a prevalent pictorial image of female hysteria [Showalter, 1987, pp. 2, 149 ff]. The hysterical attack or fit itself was considered to be 'an equivalent of coition' [Freud, 1919a, *S.E.*, IX, 234, quoted by Laplanche, 1980, p. 196]. (...)

At the opposite end of the spectrum of the sexually foregrounded portrayal of the female hysteric, we have a fourth character, namely the Figliastra in *Sei personaggi in cerca d'autore*

(1921). In her case, sexual exhibitionism is more discreet, but nevertheless present, taking the form of a song and dance routine, which she performs in orderly mourning attire, rather than in disarray. On its own, this episode may not appear particularly significant (unless, of course, one views it as an example of the spectacle of the female body, clothed or otherwise, functioning as a traditional icon of sexuality). However, when considered in its context, it acquires a special resonance. The spectacle of the Figliastra in fact disrupts the narrative, rather than promoting its progress, as she makes a bid for attention in an attempt to make her 'voice' heard in the male-dominated discourse taking place, using the discourse of the body to do so. This display must also be seen in conjunction with the element of hysteria in her behaviour. This is apparent in the manic, stridulous laughter which erupts, and interrupts, on several occasions. It functions, like her song and dance routine, as an attempt to interject her viewpoint into the discourse of the male characters, and again it takes the form of a 'muted' discourse, rather than that of effective, rational argumentation. Twice she has bouts of uncontrollable crying, with the latter of these instances followed shortly after by more stridulous laughter at the end of the play. (...)

In the face of a femininity which is culturally allied to the discourse of the body, to unreason and hysteria in all its various manifestations, any perception or representation of nervous imbalance in relation to masculinity is inherently problematic. It is therefore not surprising to find that *Enrico IV*, a play traditionally regarded as Pirandello's masterpiece on insanity, is in fact a multiple denial of male madness. This denial is effected in several ways. Firstly, and most importantly, Enrico's twelve-year long madness was not a functional disturbance of the nervous system which had its origins in a psychic conflict of any kind. Significantly, it had a purely organic, physical cause, namely a blow to the nape of the neck when he fell from his horse. Showalter's account of early twentieth-century theories of actual male hysteria resulting from traumatic experiences during the Great War, shows that medical authorities were reluctant to believe any cause other than an organic one such as 'physical injury to the brain or the central nervous system' [Showalter, 1987, p. 169]. It was culturally unacceptable, a trespassing of gender boundaries, for nervous disorder to disturb the masculine stereotype, except as the result of some external, physical phenomenon. In effect, the nape of the neck, where the spinal cord housing the central nervous system is particularly exposed, is the perfect place for such an injury to be inflicted. In other words, Enrico's madness is constructed in such a way as to pre-empt any implication of unmanly nervous disorder/hysteria/femininity. His madness is made to originate outside himself, as an accident rather than a 'natural' product of his biology.

The second element in the play's denial of male madness is that Enrico is not actually mad during the course of the play, since his madness passed away some eight years before. (...)

The 'patient', furthermore, expounds on, and condones, madness, with lengthy, rational speeches. This in itself again serves to place the male character at a safe remove from the condition itself. Male madness is thus staged as a form of self-reflexive super-rationality, in marked contrast to the uncontrolled discourse of the body which characterizes his female counterparts. The conscious theatricality of Enrico's pretended madness therefore parodies the unconscious theatricality of the female hysterics. The play, in effect, is a parody, and denial, of madness.

—Maggie Günsberg, "Hysteria as Theatre: Pirandello's Hysterical Women," *Yearbook of the Society for Pirandello Studies* 12 (Modern Drama, 1992): 32–52.

JEROME MAZZARO ON HISTORY AND MENTAL DYSFUNCTION

[Jerome Mazzaro was a Professor of Modern Languages and Literatures for over 30 years at the University of Buffalo. In his prolific career, he has published numerous essays on Pirandello's work. He is also the author of *Transformations in the Renaissance English Lyric* (Cornell

University Press, 1970) and *William Carlos Williams:The Later Poems* (Cornell University Press, 1973).]

In *Enrico IV*, Luigi Pirandello takes up these physiological and psychological functions of memory as they illuminate a number of concerns: illusion and reality, form and life, rationality and irrationality, and the nature of identity. In so doing, he, too, employs dysfunction to examine normal behavior. In the play, the particular memory dysfunctions which he uses are amnesia, or the loss of memory, and schizophrenia, a confusing, distancing, and paralyzing division of self bordering at times on paranoia and delusions of persecution and grandeur. The two dysfunctions are discrete and, as Thomas Bishop remarks in the case of amnesia, scientifically not always handled soundly. Amnesia, for example, "does not involve loss of time perception on a scale so enormous that centuries are involved."[5] Injured in a fall from a horse during a carnival twenty years before, the play's protagonist, Henry, loses his identity for twelve years. Upon recovering his memory, he finds that he no longer fits into the changed world and chooses to preserve the illusion of a fantasy one. His actions are played off against those of other characters with normal memory functions so that memory dysfunction never becomes normative or even preferable except perhaps as a purposive escape from fixity or stagnation. The presence of his contrary world in what is expected sets off the drama's deeper issues and a conceptive doubling in which art, costumes, and portraits serve as conventional *aides-memoires* or tokens to remind audiences and characters who they are or are not. (...)

It is not impossible, then to suppose that historical analogues besides the obvious ones pertaining to the real Henry IV might also be present in *Enrico IV*. If so, these analogues may well involve the equally contemporary person of another Kaiser—William II. (...)

Indeed, it is by thinking historically that Pirandello establishes the bases of his skepticism and relativism. Whereas man lives forward, his understanding of life is backward. It occurs in memories whose present impressions are ordered in terms of simultaneity or sequentiality along the lines of similarity, contrast, contiguity, and cause-and-effect. These "lines" become the "causes" or "explanations" or "truths" of the present and "models for projecting the future. (...)

In *Enrico IV*, this tendency to think historically is especially noticeable in Pirandello's handlings of memory dysfunction and personality development. Like Freud, he tends "to treat psychological facts as belonging, not to the natural order, to be investigated according to the methodologies of chemistry and biology, but to the historical order."[15] As a result, the history of Henry's memory dysfunctions and the dysfunctions become joined. (...)

The play's major memory dysfunctions appear as discontinuity. Not only is there Henry's unwillingness to carry past verbal experience into the present, but there are also his abrupt time and place shifts and inability to relate to others and the play's impersonal suggestions and withholdings of exact likeness. (...)

In the case of Henry, the discontinuity becomes for audiences evidence of near mock, or real madness, especially as it exists coevally with noticeable behavioral fixations and delusions. By their positioning, the abrupt formal swings, turns, and "doublings" that do not double make possible associative binary relationships and the "dynamic life" conditions for the play's exchanges and opportunistic turns. They make possible, for example, the "doubling" of the marchesa as she was and as she is and the false "doubling" of her daughter as the marchesa was at the time of the accident. They likewise allow the "doublings" of the mad and sane Henry and the marquis and Henry as well as, for audiences, the double plots of the play's action, the doublings of art and life, and the "doublings" of the young men as servants and counsellors. The normal effects of such doubling is intelligibility and a revivification of the past through subjective clarification and reinforcement. In *Enrico IV*, these effects give way to a questioning or canceling action. Intelligibility is undermined rather than enhanced and, as in absurdist drama, audiences are left to respond principally to the work's abstract, pythagorean, mathematical, "significant," or formal attributes.

Critics are generally agreed that, despite the presence of credible symptoms, Henry is not mad in any standard clinical sense. (...)

Pirandello's historical thinking does not permit him to believe in a permanent external Great Memory on whose fringes individual memories collect and to which, through symbols, great art makes its timeless appeal. Like Hegel, who considers modern Christianity superior to that of Church Fathers by virtue of historical change, Pirandello considers the present to be different enough from the past that the past cannot truthfully be "a way of controlling, of ordering, of giving a shape and a significance to the immense panorama of futility and anarchy which is contemporary history."[24] Therefore there can be none of the "eternal return" which Nietzsche promotes in *Thus Spoke Zarathustra* (1883) nor, despite the play's close adherence to dramatic unities, meaning simply through the execution of aesthetic form. Critics who have tried to base interpretations and order on either historical or artistic precedents are soon defeated. Contemporary anarchy is not controlled or significantly illuminated by its historical precedents. Indeed, if anything the precedents make clear that, like *Enrico IV*'s structural doublings, history does not repeat itself exactly. Similarly, while superficially suggesting escapist play elements with costumes, time shifts, and playing at roles, the action gains life by its violations of rather than its subscriptions to dramatic rules. Still, there is enough adherence to history to bring out the drama's deviations from life and enough softening of daydream and adherence to "purely formal or aesthetic pleasure" to preserve a "consciousness of fiction."[25]

To a great degree the success of productions of *Enrico IV* depends on the ability of the actor playing the title role to win over audiences. It is he on whom the action centers and who must suggest continuity in discontinuity, sincerity among all the action's playing at roles, and a credible human being beneath all the intellectual play. Critics have pointed out how unsympathetic and seductive the role at times is. Henry is bitter, sadistic, and self-centered. (...)

In responding to the play, audiences consequently cannot ignore the possibility that it may present a model for or allegory of one of Ribot's organizing centers or nodes. The villa offers interior space into which the visitors, like impressions from without, intrude and are ultimately absorbed, reshaped, integrated, and, in the instance of Belcredi, destroyed by Henry's "creative madness." Like memory, the play, as Paolucci points out, "consists of compulsive attempts to piece together broken continuities of time, reason, love, relationships, historical fact, and present fiction." It "is the epitome of *personality*." Still, as Freud might argue, it is a center or node whose ego functions appear to have been damaged. They have been cut off from Bergson's central switchboard to the detriment of not only memory's own cognitive functions but also the evaluative and regulatory actions of the superego. Unchecked, the forces of the id have increased to the point that Henry and the play do not seem to know how to end, and indeed within the villa death may be the only ending. Henry will continue there insane. Yet events have occurred which have turned that prospect for audiences into unsatisfactory pretense—"an illusion of illusion.... Not only can [Henry] no longer dream of being cut loose from his [role of] Emperor, he cannot even live as Emperor either, for the attendants no longer believe him mad." For Michel Serres, whose views in this instance may lie closer to Pirandello's, the visitors are "noise" which in Henry's failure to integrate into a dynamic, larger cognitive system dooms him and his world to stasis, marginality, incompleteness, and madness.[28] Like the scientific work on memory dysfunction, the play from the failure seeks insights into unimpaired memory workings.

5. Thomas Bishop, *Pirandello and the French Theater* (New York: New York Univ. Press, 1966), p. 27.

15. W. H. Auden, "The Greatness of Freud," *Listener*, 50 (1953), 593. For Pirandello and Freud, see Luigi Russo, "Pirandello e la psicoanalisi," in *Pirandello e la cultura del suo tempo*, ed. Stefano Milioto and Enzo Scrivano (Milan: Mursia, 1984), pp. 31–54; Eric Bentley, "Il Tragico Imperatore," *Tulane Drama Review*, 10, No. 3 (1966); 60–75; and Douglas Biow, "Psychoanalysis, History, Marginality: A Study of Violence and Disease in Pirandello's *Enrico IV*," *Italica*, 66 (1989), 158–75. See also Arminio Janner, *Luigi Pirandello* (Florence: Nuova Italia, 1958), pp. 10–15; André Bouissy, "Réflexions sur l'histoire et la pré-histoire du personnage 'alter ego'," in *Lectures Pirandelliennes* (Abbeville: F. Paillart, 1978), pp. 101–74; and Anthony Caputi, *Pirandello and the Crisis of Modern Consciousness* (Urbana: Univ. of Illinois Press, 1988).

24. T. S. Eliot, "Ulysses, Order, and Myth," *The Dial*, 75 (1923), 483.

25. Sigmund Freud, "Creative Writers and Daydreaming," in *Critical Theory Since Plato*, ed. Hazard Adams (New York: Harcourt Brace Jovanovich, 1971), p. 753. Bentley, for example, sees the murder of Belcredi as necessitated less by tragic form than by "Sicilian melodrama—or opera libretto, if you will—of love, jealousy, and revenge" ("Il Tragico Imperatore," p. 66) and doubts a successful division in Pirandello's illusion/reality distinctions. Starkie, questioning the timing of Henry's revelation of his sanity, notes that "from a dramatic point of view there does not seem to be any need for him to tell his servants at that particular point in the play.... The episode seems to be dragged in to provide a fine climax to the second act" (*Luigi Pirandello*, pp. 190–91). Other critics have argued the appropriateness of the play's structure being labeled "a tragedy" and the kind of tragedy which it may suggest. The play's deliberately jarring anachronisms have already been mentioned.

28. Paolucci, *Pirandello's Theater*, pp. 98, 101; Bentley, "Il Tragico Imperatore," pp. 74–75; Michel Serres, *The Parasite*, trans. Lawrence R. Schehr (Baltimore: Johns Hopkins Univ. Press, 1982).

—Jerome Mazzaro, "Memory and Madness in Pirandello's *Enrico IV*," *Comparative Drama* 26:1 (1992): 34–57

Tonight We Improvise

Tonight We Improvise begins with an audience shouting, apparently as angry as the audience was at the end of the first staging of *Six Characters*—except that the angry spectators in this instance are actors who are among the audience as a part of the play's action. This allows Dr. Hinkfuss, the director, an arena in which to indignantly present at some length his theatrical doctrine. Hinkfuss is a grotesque, a physical reflection that Pirandello accords him because of directors' conviction that they rank foremost as responsible for a play's success rather than playwrights or actors. Described as no taller than an arm's length with long, long hair, he has hands that repulse, his fingers so covered with hair that they resemble caterpillars more than anything else, the entirety of appearance intended obviously to image Pirandello's opinion of directors. Hinkfuss perceives that only under his "fine hand" does a play emerge from a playwright's crude form to assume shape and meaning. Max Reinhardt, who had brilliantly directed *Six Characters*, and of whom Pirandello thought highly, has been designated the probable model for Hinkfuss. Pirandello manages to express both his admiration for Reinhardt and disdain for directors in simultaneously undermining and exalting the value of the director's role. Dr. Hinkfuss's doctrine is engaging and the scene itself humorous as the actors in the audience and Hinkfuss interact. An audience might be amused and intrigued by the "audience actors'" antics, moved by Sampognetta's death, and then later by Mommina's, but its confusion would not be very much relieved.

The basic events of the play are simple: the father of a family dies, leaving a mother and four daughters. Whereas their life before has been looked down upon by their Sicilian community because it has consisted of drinking (mostly the father) and enjoying often the company of air force officers (the mother and daughters), it becomes even worse at the father's death since they are without the money he could provide. The oldest daughter

Mommina sacrifices her promising operatic career by marrying an air force officer, who reveals himself as a frighteningly jealous man after the marriage. She had thought to improve her family's fortune, but her marriage accomplishes only sorrow for her and no improvement for her family.

The action opens with a religious procession that moves with some state, bells playing, across the stage; then jazz replaces their sound as they move off. A nightclub scene emerges; though behind a thin curtain, the audience can see the black-clad singer and a kind of focus on one member of her audience, the Old Comic Actor who plays the role of Sampognetta. Drunk, he weeps at the singer's song. Would-be comedians have cut horns out of paper and dropped them over his hat; he laughs when the pranksters laugh, unaware that he is their joke. The singer pities the old man because they make sport of him and his drunkenness; the old man listens with devotion to her, thinking she sounds like Mommina and may once have also sacrificed a better life to support her siblings and parents.

Sampognetta is ousted from the nightclub just at the moment his wife and daughters are passing on their way to the opera. The mother's sarcasm almost brings about a fight. Dr. Hinkfuss reappears to assist in the scene change to the opera; his appearance reiterates to an audience that this is an improvised play, as does the confusion that ensues at the opera as the mother Ignazia and the daughters enter late because of the fracas in the street. The intermission at the opera occurs simultaneously with the intermission of the play itself, and the players and audience move about together, discussing what has happened. The characters remain in role; there are no revelations about anything, just chat. Hinkfuss creates an airport on the stage; an improvisation perhaps on his part, but he dismantles it as soon as it is completed.

When the play resumes, Ignazia is trying to cure a toothache with prayer. Her daughter Totina comes in singing to help her mother forget her pain. Mommina enters after a time and also sings to distract her mother's toothache. Verri then comes with medicine for Ignazia and becomes furious when he hears Mommina singing. The scene, now quite crowded with daughters and airmen, degenerates into disorder and confusion in the play's movement. Mommina says a line too soon and Verri becomes angry at her error. Personal tension is added to the chaos of improvisation and liberty becomes license.

Sampognetta arrives, wearing blood all over. He has been knocking, knocking, trying to get in so that he can die, but no one has heard him in the noise of their arguments over improvisation. The actors respect the movement of a play, and they cease their arguments so that he may enter for his scene. The storyline is that he has been injured in his fight to support his beloved singer at the nightclub. They are puzzled, however, that he is smiling. His explanation is that they are all better than he is. Hinkfuss gets up in irritation to stop the Old Comic Actor from going on with this, but he insists that he cannot stop laughing. The maid was to let him in and tell the others that he was being carried home dying, but in the pandemonium among the characters, she didn't do this. Hinkfuss says that it doesn't matter, he is inside now. So he can go ahead and die.

Sampognetta lies down on the couch, saying, "I'm dead," which Hinkfuss does not like. The Old Comic Actor then gets up to explain that Hinkfuss should finish him off because he cannot die without an entrance that covers some part of the situation leading to it. There were things to be said, actions to make the act comprehensible and matter, and to make the connection between the revelry of the house and his exile into fooldom. He had a role to play as a drunk and as a sad man. Now he will call up an audience member and between the stranger and the singer, with his chin on the singer's breast, he will die.

The Old Comic Actor has so moved the audience that Dr. Hinkfuss has been forgotten. Just as the mother and daughters are about to respond to his death, Hinkfuss leaps up to stop the action (a successful one to him, but requiring no response as far as he is concerned) and move to strike the scene, take down the lights, set the next scene.

As the actors change for the next scene, Hinkfuss discusses (for the audience's enlightenment) the disagreement he and the Leading Actress have in the interpretation of Mommina. This functions as a preparation for those of the audience who have not understood how crass Hinkfuss has been. The actors return to the stage unwilling to continue unless Hinkfuss leaves. Improvisation has provided freedom and creation of art that closely resembles reality, but they perceive Hinkfuss as incapable of relinquishing his need to make puppets of his actors. The audience has seen, however, the chaos that ignored the scene that was to lead up to the Old Comic Actor Sampognetta's death and the near jettisoning of it, saved only by his ability to improvise. Thus improvisation can create art very like life, but art still requires control or it becomes life in its impetuosity rather than art. He leaves, or so they think.

The Character Actress mother accomplishes the aging of Mommina, the actress's change in appearance that changes the character. Mommina then establishes that the walls create her prison, going to each and saying "This is wall—This is wall—This is wall." Verri has narrowed her life to one single room in his jealousy that would not allow her to express herself in singing nor even with her family. The play ends with Mommina and her children, as she tells them of theater and opera in an effort to open that world to them. But she dies trying to sing the Azucena aria from Verdi's *Il Trovatore*.

Her mother, sisters, and Verri are about to begin their response to her death when Hinkfuss runs forward from the back of the theater, praising them for creating the scene so well. He tells them that he never left the theater, but rather involved himself in creating the lighting, underscoring perhaps the theatrical expression, "It's all in how you light it." The audience has been unaware of it, but the lighting directions have been a part of the progression of Mommina's decline, its art enhancing and further dramatizing the most significant scene. Hinkfuss has, nonetheless, interrupted a point of genuine continuity, as well as distracted them from Mommina, who lies still on the stage. Fainting because of her immersion in her role, she lies before them in what the Old Comic Actor calls a danger of improvisation. Hinkfuss does not agree, though he says he will use a script but with the liberty to have improvisation. The play ends on an indecisive note.

Tonight We Improvise

Dr. Hinkfuss is an amalgam of the kind of director that Pirandello hated and the kind that he love and respected, thus Hinkfuss is a contradiction of sorts. He presents a long doctrinaire statement that is admirable, but he will not follow it in his direction of the play. He is an advocate of improvisation, but he cannot relinquish his control of the actors.

Old Comic Actor plays Sampognetta, a drunk who has fathered four daughters and leaves them and his wife bereft with his death. The characters are both the actors and the characters.

Character Actress plays Donna Ignazia, is the mother of the family and just as fond as her daughters for entertaining air force men.

Leading Lady plays Mommina. Her character sacrifices her operatic career for her family and gains little to nothing in the bargain. Her husband imprisons her in effect, and no great financial help is provided for her mother and sisters.

Leading Man plays Verri, Mommina's husband. He is jealous, violent, and has closed down her life by confining her to one single room. He will not even allow her to sing, and her music dies within her.

Tonight We Improvise

SUSAN BASSNETT-MCGUIRE ON HINKFUSS AS THEATRICAL NEGATOR

[Susan Bassnett-McGuire, Professor in the Comparative Literature Department at the University of Warwick in England, has written on Sylvia Plath, Elizabeth I, and Bernhardt, Terry, and Duse, in addition to Pirandello.]

Much of the comedy in the play comes from the clashes between Hinkfuss and the actors, who finally succeed in throwing him out only to have him reappear to claim the credit at the end. Hinkfuss as a director is pompous, wordy, arrogant and overly ambitious; he has been seen as Pirandello's satire on the exaggerated power enjoyed by such directors as Pitoëff and Reinhardt. (...)

[W]hen the actors unite to get rid of him, they point out in no uncertain terms that his presence is useless:

THE LEADING ACTOR: Real theatre!
THE COMIC ACTOR: What you chuck away every night! Your idea of theatre is just giving people something flashy to look at.
THE CHARACTER ACTRESS: When you live out a feeling, that's real theatre; then all you need is the odd prop.
THE LEADING LADY: You can't play around with feelings.
THE LEADING ACTOR: You can only juggle everything for effects if   you're dealing with petty comedies.
ALL THE OTHERS: Get out.
DR. HINKFUSS: I am your director.
THE LEADING ACTOR: Life can't be directed by anyone when it's coming into being.

In this central scene we see the strength of Pirandello's views on theatre, repeatedly expressed in his theoretical writings. Theatre, he argues, through the Actors, is not artificially created great effects, it is a quasi-mystical moment of fusion between life and the play. As the play develops the actor lives his part for the period of time that it takes for the play to run its course. It is not too difficult to see the links between Pirandello's idea of life for a character and Stanislawski's notion of the actor absorbing the role he plays, while his attack on the exaggerations of spectacle theatre point to his sympathy for a theatre of flesh and blood rather than a theatre of high technique. (...)

Hinkfuss is the personification of everything that Pirandello sees as negative in theatre, he is an anti-theatre force. (...)

In the clash between Hinkfuss and the actors, we see exemplified the clash between the absolute and the relative. Hinkfuss wants to impose order even on improvization, everything must be defined and conform to his vision. The actors demand the freedom to allow chance impressions and unprogrammed action to happen without a predetermined pattern: that is, they demand to bring characters to life. But when, at the end of the play, Hinkfuss reappears to claim the credit, and we hear that he has been secretly controlling the lighting effects, we can see that the actors have only a very limited kind of freedom, restricted by the stage, the audience and above all by the fact that they are reproducing other lives. (...)

The actor can only reproduce reality within the limits set by theatre. Once an actor feels real pain or actually dies, he is no longer acting. The actors' revolt cannot ultimately succeed, because they demand the freedom of life within the constrictions of theatre and this is impossible. At the same time, Pirandello is using the theatre, as he so often does, as a metaphor for life. Ultimate freedom, whether to leave the stage or to leave life through death, is negation. (...)

In the preface to *Six Characters* Pirandello expresses his contempt for the kind of theatre Hinkfuss tries to create, and the stage directions of *Tonight We Improvise* repeat that feeling. In Act

II, Pirandello's stage directions tell us that Hinkfuss 'starts to beat about the bush' when he creates his elaborate Sicilian procession; this comic commentary on Hinkfuss' theatre practice increases during the Intermission scenes, at times becoming quite heavy-handed. (...)

The ambiguity that Pirandello seems to have felt for spectacle theatre is apparent in *Tonight We Improvise*. Hinkfuss may be mocked and temporarily defeated by the actors, but he is also the figure who has some profound things to say about the nature of theatre. His elaborate stage effects are satirized, but the problem of their effectiveness remains, and the Sicilian procession, seen without the frame of Pirandello's derisory stage directions, can be an effective *coup de théâtre*. Moreover, although the Actors argue the case for a poor theatre, where stage effects and props take second place, the use of lighting in key moments such as Mommina's death scene is by no means a cheap trick but an important contribution to the final effect.

What seems to be happening in *Tonight We Improvise* is that Pirandello is debating with himself about the nature of theatre. Opposed in principle to spectacle theatre, he was also fascinated by it, and was sufficiently involved with practical theatre to understand the exigencies placed on a director. The satire against Hinkfuss is primarily directed against his attempts to control everything that happens, to use his position to exert power over the actors and to manipulate the audience. Hinkfuss attempts to shape into his own mould that which Pirandello argues is a fluid process. (...)

Tonight We Improvise is a huge panoramic play about theatre making. It presents a wide range of angles to the problems of the amount of control that can and should be exerted over the processes of bringing theatre into being; on another level it presents the problem of the relativity of the freedom of mankind. 'Freedom and peace can only be had if one pays the price of ceasing to live', says Hinkfuss early in the play; in this case no-one ever can be free while still alive. Man is imprisoned in life, in the same way as the actor is confined to the stage in order to 'live'. (...)

The plays of the theatre trilogy each develop one aspect of the processes of making a play: *Six Characters* focuses on the problem of the relationship between author, characterization in the written text and characterization in the performance text. *Each in His Own Way* focuses on the problem of the relationship between the play (in the playing the distinction between written and performance texts is blurred) and the audience, while *Tonight We Improvise* focuses on the problem of the creation of that performance text. What emerges strongly and clearly from all three plays is that Pirandello perceives theatre in dialectical terms, a series of dynamic relationships with no element being more or less significant than any other. Theatre is a process, it is the result of a set of separate and very different systems, each of equal importance. In his essay 'Theatre and Literature' (1918) Pirandello distinguishes between the idea of theatre that devalues the written text to the level of a *commedia dell'arte* scenario and one where the written text is treated seriously as part of the total process. In this essay he comes remarkably close to some of the views on theatre being formulated in the 20s and 30s in Russia and Czechoslovakia, among the groups later referred to as the Russian Formalists and Prague Structuralists. In his insistence on theatre as a dialectical set of relationships Pirandello might well be described as a theatre semiotician.

—Susan Bassnett-McGuire, *Luigi Pirandello* (Grove Press, 1983): 56–70.

ANTHONY CAPUTI ON MELDING SCRIPT AND IMPROVISATION

[Anthony Caputi spent the entirety of his career teaching Dramatic Literature and Creative Writing at Cornell University. His publications include *John Marston, Satirist* and *Buffo, the Genius of Vulgar Comedy*, as well as articles on Shakespeare and modern drama.]

What is new in *Tonight We improvise*, and what sets it off from *Each in His Own Way* and *Six Characters*, is its emphasis on creation as a confused collaboration. As explained by Hinkfuss, the actors bring movement to the fixed outline of the story, which Hinkfuss compares to a sculpture: they theatricalize it and in that way create experience. Their efforts, depending on your point of view, are helped or hindered by the director and his backstage aides. What is most important from our point of view is that the creation at issue be seen as the product of many individuals at once contending with each other and yet cooperating, quarreling, taking and giving offence, sulking, and rebelling, even as they are all propelled forward by the events of the outline story. Moreover, we are in a position to see that this image of Hinkfuss's actors making a play is mirrored both in the efforts of Pirandello's actors to theatricalize his text and in those of the characters in the "improvised" play to perform scenes from operas, especially *Il Trovatore*. Seen as a totality, then, *Tonight We Improvise* consists of interpenetrating theatricalizations: Pirandello's actors are performing the written script of a play in which actors "improvise" a play in which the characters in turn put on amateur versions of opera. The ensemble of these efforts is disorderly, even clumsy and inept, and it is held together by the purpose of giving form to experience that would otherwise remain a chaos of contending voices. The action reveals not simply that the process of creation, scenic or otherwise, is messy, but that messiness, hence precariousness, is intrinsic to it. Actors putting on a play can serve as an emblem of the process by which experience is created through theatricalization; but actors improvising a play stress the dominant quality of that process, its chanciness, the wonder that the play ever gets put on at all. The further implication, of course, is that all this is true not simply of what Hinkfuss calls scenic creation, but also of self-creation.

Of the trilogy of theater plays *Tonight We Improvise* is the most loosely structured. The distinctive planes of theatricalization do not collide in it as in *Six Characters* or *Each in His Own Way*: they overlap and dribble into each other. The actors' awkward first steps into improvisation, as when, for example, the mother mismatches the suitors with her daughters, or the actors break into the action to object or complain that something has been changed or omitted, or the sisters and mother appear surrealistically in the long scene between Mommina, the prosecuted sister, and her mad Sicilian husband who, stepping out of his role of the husband and speaking as the actor, protests that they are not literally there: all this strengthens the sense of 'indeterminacy' in the action, even as excursions into *Il Trovatore* sustain an obbligato of overwrought intensity. When the actors rebel and drive Hinkfuss off, their gesture marks merely a further stage in a process that sporadically threatens to become wholly anarchic. But it never does. Hinkfuss returns and the collaboration resumes with Hinkfuss's promise that texts may be provided, as the actors are demanding, though not an author or indeed anything that might hobble spontaneity. This temporary truce between director and actors affirms that creation will continue, always open and uncertain, like an improvised performance, and always governed by the theatrical matrix.

Finally, understanding the place of theatricality in experience serves, like understanding the other dimensions of consciousness, to bring imaginative depth and density to self-creation. To live with a full awareness of the theatricality of experience is to accept the perpetual tension between the impulses to live and theatrical forms, to acquiesce in the fact that the role you play is never entirely your own and never completely adequate to the self of your consciousness. Settling for this compromise does not compromise *sincerità*: it is in the nature of *sincerità* that it comprehends the necessity of partial measures; but it recognizes the ironic heroism of playing a role at all, a heroism caught wonderfully by Chiarchiaro of "The License," the character who demands that he be licensed as a "hexer" because that is how people insist on seeing him. To live with these awarenesses is to clarify the extremely delicate exercise of sustaining the tension between the immediate, with its flawed opportunities for living, and everything the mind brings to bear on it.

—Anthony Caputi, "The Theatrical Matrix of Experience," *Pirandello and the Crisis of Modern Consciousness* (University of Illinois Press, 1988): 120–23.

OLGA RAGUSA ON PIRANDELLO'S DRAMA AS EVOLVING *COMMEDIA DELL'ARTE*

[Olga Ragusa is Da Ponte Professor of Italian Emerita and former chair of the department at Columbia University. In 1998 she was given the distinction of "Ufficiale" in the order of merit of the Italian republic by the President of Italy. She has published *Pirandello: An Approach to His Theatre* (Edinburgh University Press, 1980) and *Luigi Pirandello* (Columbia University Press, 1980).]

The title of the play, whether in Italian or English or other languages into which it has been translated, refers to a type of theater, *commedia dell'arte*, which rose to great popularity in the sixteenth and seventeenth centuries but had been completely replaced on the legitimate stage by the nineteenth. The creation of actors, of tightly knit acting companies in which the "art," the know-how, was handed down from father to son, from mother to daughter, *commedia dell'arte* constitutes Italy's greatest contribution to the European comic tradition. With its scenarios, its masks, and its repertories of lines, it is recalled in the introductory note to *Tonight We Improvise* (p. 226).[4] Its inner dynamics for the actor, the strains it puts on the actor, are illustrated by the Character Actress when she objects that she cannot "pretend" to slap the Old Comic Actor. She must actually slap him, because in the absence of a written part, "it must all come from here (and she makes a gesture from the stomach upward)" (238–39). The company called on to perform in *Tonight We Improvise* is not accustomed to acting in this manner, and its rebellion off and onstage in Part I results from its encounter in a devalued setting (that of a play without a script) of the principle of *immedesimarsi*, to identify with, which Pirandello postulates elsewhere as the very key to artistic creation.[5]

Whereas in a conventional play we might have expected to speak of characters with names and fully rounded make-believe identities and personalities, we have instead been speaking of actors designated only by their roles. Like the *commedia dell'arte* style of recitation, insistence on the dichotomy between actor and character is a novelty in *Tonight We Improvise*, although this one, too, is not an absolute one in the Pirandello *corpus*. The reader or the spectator turns to the "Cast of Characters" for *Six Characters, Each in His Own Way*, and *The Mountain Giants* and finds that in all three cases a distinction is being made—even typographically—between two groups: between the "Characters of the play to be made" and the "Actors of the company" in the first instance, between "Characters fixed in the role of the play on stage" and "Temporary, occasional characters in the theater lobby" in the second, and between the "Characters in the Countess's company" and the "Scaglionati," characters who act for the magician Cotrone (among whom are puppets, apparitions, and even an angel) in the third. In each case, although the distinction is specific to the particular play, the contrast is one of essence. It is the very being, the ontological status, of the opposed groups that is at issue. In *Tonight We Improvise* the fact of the distinction, which it took Pirandello so much effort in *Six Characters* to establish and demonstrate in an easily perceivable fashion, is taken as a given. So much so that the division into groups has disappeared. The Character Actress, the Old Comic Actor, the Leading Actor, and the Leading Actress not only play the roles assigned to them, but they *have become* those roles: they *are* Signora Ignazia, Sampognetta, Rico Verri, Mommina. This fusion between actor and character for the duration of a performance is usual in the accepted illusion of reality on stage, but in Pirandello the experience for the spectator is destabilizing because it is forced on his consciousness. In *Tonight We Improvise* the process by which a character is created on stage (not in its author's imagination as in the Preface to *Six Characters*) is made visible as the actors begin to be introduced to the audience physically, in their bodily consistency (not as printed marks on a page). But they insist on being presented instead as the characters they are playing, the characters they are "making" life and blood.

The characters are "introduced": the very use of the

expression implies that there is someone to do the introducing, a kind of master of ceremonies, who is distinct from the actors or actors-turned-characters. Such a one is Doctor Hinkfuss, whose name is the only one appearing on the manifesto that announces the performance. Such would also be the voice of the author in narrative. We come to another characteristic of *Tonight We Improvise*, another novelty for reader and spectator: the narrative quality of the play, the blurring of the lines between storytelling and story-acted-out. Both drama and narrative are representational forms, and the techniques of the one are often found in the other. It should come as no surprise that in a writer as prolific as Pirandello in both genres there should be instances of confusion between them, an instinctive, spontaneous slipping in and out of what is in theory separate. But because drama and literary criticism have in the heyday of theater rarely been entrusted to the same person, it took some time for the process by which this occurs to be pinpointed and analyzed.[6] As in *Each in His Own Way* (whose revised edition was subsequent to the premier of *Tonight We Improvise*) so in *Tonight We Improvise* the play begins with a description, which then quickly turns into an acted-out demonstration, of circumstances prior to the action on stage. The stage is set, as it were, but it is not the traditional stage with its missing fourth wall. The focus, instead, is on the audience: on why they are there, on what their expectations are, on what the reactions of the critics will probably be, on the hubbub and excitement, the self-satisfaction and the fault-finding of the public as it looks forward to and is at the same time distrustful of what the evening will bring. Once Hinkfuss enters the theater, he takes over, quelling the tumult with his authority. But the narrator's voice is back at the end of the Intermezzo when the stage directions expand into a multifaceted commentary on Hinkfuss's novel way of making theater, a built-in vindication of Pirandello's own "improvised" play (267–68). The stage directions, in other words, which are normally atypical in Pirandello because they go well beyond telling an actor where to stand and what to do, here reveal their origin in the narrator's point of view. Pirandello did not stop being a storyteller when he took up drama. In his lifelong quest for ever more direct and effective communication, his storytelling grew into drama; it did not replace it.

The presence of a narrative dimension and its impact on the play may be more easily perceived by the reader than the spectator of *Tonight We Improvise*. But no one can miss the exploitation of theatrical media other than the stage, and together with the radical enlargement of acting space, it is indeed the most striking novelty of this play.

NOTES

4. Since the volume of the critical edition of *Maschere nude* slated to include *Questa sera si recita a soggetto* has not yet been published, references in this chapter are to the standard edition listed under Works Cited. Translations throughout are the present writer's, although there are two translations of the play into English.

5. For some instances, see Ragusa, *Luigi Pirandello*, by referring to the entry "*immedesimarsi*" in the Index.

6. See Jansen, "Struttura narrativa," for an analysis with regard to the stage directions.

—Olga Ragusa, "*Tonight We Improvise:* Spectacle and Tragedy," *A Companion to Pirandello Studies* (Greenwood Press, 1991): 245–258.

JAMES FISHER ON PIRANDELLO'S PERVASIVE KNOWLEDGE AND USE OF *COMMEDIA DELL'ARTE*

[James Fisher, Professor of Theater at Wabash College, has published on the history of *commedia dell'arte* in the twentieth century. In addition to writing about Pirandello and the theater, he has published books on Al Jolson, Spencer Tracy, and Eddie Cantor.]

Commedia dell'arte was the rarest of theatrical forms—a non-literary theatre that emphasized the skill of the improvising actor. Commedia actors transformed human frailty into incisive satire as they literally created a play before the audience's eyes from a simple scenario. The popularity of commedia grew over the centuries as the forms and characters it inspired evolved, supplying diverse and delightful entertainments throughout Europe's theatres. In many cultures, these commedic forms offered a style of ritualized carnival—a popular street theatre that served not only as communal fun, but also as a political instrument through its ever present satire and mockery of the powerful. This seemingly casual and lowly form of theatre became a distinctly powerful *lingua franca* of the imagination, connecting cultures and artists throughout Europe. Like the best and rarest forms of theatre, commedia was both spiritual and intellectual. It proved to be universally malleable and national, adapting in each country where it appeared to the needs of that culture's artists and audiences. (...)

Pirandello's view of commedia was, it seems, highly individual, based less on a scholarly knowledge of commedia's history than on a basic and profoundly intuitive understanding of its characters, scenarios, and acting style. Placing extraordinary characters in absurd and densely complex situations with impossible resolutions delighted Pirandello. His plays, as commedia scenarios do, create surprising and fantastic situations that seem too complex to unravel. He manages a return to the ordinary through his magical ability to resolve the complicated contradictions and through flights into commedia-style farce. Pirandello's finest works are mature and polished *literary* achievements, not rough spontaneous commedia scenarios, yet he depends heavily on the skill of the athletic and improvisatory actor and an illusion of spontaneity, in true commedia fashion. *Right You Are, If You Think You Are* (1917), *Six Characters in Search of An Author* (1921), *Henry IV* (1922), and *Tonight We Improvise* (1929), will fall as flat as any uninspired commedia scenario in the hands of uninventive actors.

Pirandello hoped to introduce new methods of theatrical production in Italy similar to those he had discovered in other European cultures. He was fascinated by puppets, having been familiar with traditional Sicilian puppets since boyhood. He also advocated the use of actual masks, but, more often, employed stylized make-up and lighting effects instead of actual masks in his productions. The mask supplied him with a tangible symbol for the conflict between illusion and reality, the issue at the core of his plays. Masks were both protective and destructive to him, and they served as metaphors, as well as theatrical devices in his plays. To Pirandello, the mask was a disguise, a way of hiding or obscuring truth and creating a shifting sense of reality. Reality did not necessarily hide behind a single mask, for to Pirandello everything was masked: "Masks, they are all masks, a puff and they are gone, to make room for others masks."[5] (...)

He focused on a reform of acting that included experimentation with commedia performance techniques, especially improvisation. He saw the author, rather than the actor, as the true theatrical creator, despite his belief that "many bad plays have become excellent by what the actors have created and thus have triumphed on stage!"[8] (...)

Pirandello saw commedia as an inheritance of Roman comedy, as part of a tradition, and not as a national naive form as so many more sentimental commentators have seen it. By the time commedia had reached its peak, it had developed as "a quicker and more prudent way, certainly a more decisive way, of profiting from all the material of classical comedy,"[27] from the ancients through Ruzzante and his contemporaries. Commedia provided internationally acclaimed entertainment because the Italian theatre had, above all others, "drained the recovered classical world of all that it had to offer."[28] Pirandello claimed that the triumph of theatre throughout Europe during the Renaissance was a direct result of the influence of Italian theatre, especially commedia. (...)

Pirandello's first important full-length play, *Right You Are, If You Think You Are* (1917), appears to be as loosely constructed as a commedia scenario: thus creating the illusion of improvisation. Eric Bentley, who has translated the play, describes the play's central character, Lamberto Laudisi, a *brillante*, as "Harlequin in modern dress, a Harlequin who has invaded the realm of philosophy, and who behaves there as he had behaved elsewhere."[41] (...)

Six Characters in Search of an Author (1921) gained international celebrity for Pirandello through its exposition of both the illusion and reality inherent to theatre and to life. (...)

Depending on his experiences as a playwright and director, combined with his despairing but compassionate view of human nature and art, Pirandello makes use of his understanding of commedia-style improvisation to create and recreate the complex relationships of his emblematic characters. Caught up in the complex tangles of life, his "actors" and "characters" are ordinary people he uses as types, but like the characters of commedia they seem to have free expressions and movements that even their author did not give them. They also suggest commedia masks: the Stepdaughter is the *inamorata*, the Father is Pantalone, and the Actors and Actresses are *zanni*. Pirandello succeeds at the unlikely task of combining Realism and nearly pure commedia in a single play. By using theatre as a metaphor he exposes his characters' tragedies, by breaking through the illusion of the theatre with the illusion of improvisation. (...)

In *Henry IV*, Pirandello's characters are again inspired by the masks of commedia. Frida and the nephew are the *inamorati*, Belcredi is the jealous lover, and the doctor is a semi-comic quack, resembling commedia's Dottore. Henry himself is a commedia clown, an Arlecchino, impersonating a madman. (...)

With *Tonight We Improvise* (1929), which he produced in 1930, Pirandello presents, as he did in *Six Characters in Search of an Author* and *Each in His Own Way*, an examination of how theatre is created, emphasizing the idea that theatre comes alive when it is tied directly to the imagination of the actor. (...)

Tonight We Improvise, like *Six Characters in Search of an Author* and *Each in His Own Way*, resembles commedia in its character transformations, the sudden changes of direction in the action, the conflict between the play and the play-within-the-play, and what Pirandello described as the "'aggressive vitality' of the *commedia*."[63] He also makes it clear in his plays, as in commedia, that the emphasis is on the illusion of the actors' creativity, not on any realistic happening. A feeling of urgency and spontaneity is created by the playwright, as in commedia, despite the fact that the actors work from a complete and carefully constructed script with finished dialogue. It was necessary for an actor in a Pirandello play, as A. Richard Sogliuzzo writes, to "function skillfully within these various levels of reality while appearing to be confused as to the distinctions between fact and fiction, art and life, and his identity as character or actor."[64]

NOTES

5. Cited in Jana O'Keefe Bazzoni, "The Carnival Motif in Pirandello's Drama," *Modern Drama*, 30 (1987), 421.

8. Cited in Eric Bentley, ed., "Pirandello and Performance," *Theatre Three*, 3 (Fall 1987), 70.

27. Luigi Pirandello, "Introduction to The Italian Theatre," trans. Anne Paolucci. *The Genius of the Italian Theatre*, Ed. Eric Bentley (New York, 1964), p. 25.

28. Idem.

41. Eric Bentley, *The Pirandello Commentaries* (Evanston, IL, 1984), p. 29.

63. Cited in A. Richard Sogliuzzo, *Luigi Pirandello, Director: The Playwright in the Theatre* (Metuchen, NJ, and London, 1982), p. 42.

64. Ibid., p. 43.

—James Fisher, "An Author in Search of Characters: Pirandello and Commedia dell'arte," *Modern Drama* 35: 4 (Modern Drama, 1992): 495–512.

MARVIN ROSENBERG ON PIRANDELLO'S RESPONSE TO CUMULATIVE CRITICAL ASSESSMENTS

[Marvin Rosenberg has written extensively on Shakespeare. His books include *Adventures of a Shakespeare Scholar* (1997), *Masks of Hamlet* (1992), *Masks of King Lear* (1992), *Masks of Othello* (1992), *Masks of Macbeth* (1978), and others of note.]

In all his best self-questioning plays, Pirandello's characters find that the firm selves they believe they own are in fact made up of evanescent hopes, impulses, wishes, fears, social pressures, the instincts of the animal inheritance. They are driven deeper: Pirandello tried to make them express explicitly, in his *Six Characters*—"as their own living passion and torment the passion and torment which for so many years have been the pangs of my spirit: the deceit of mutual understanding irremediably founded on the empty abstraction of words, the multiple personality of everyone corresponding to the possibilities of being found in each of us, and finally the inherent tragic conflict between life (which is always moving and changing) and form (which fixes it, immovable)." (...)

To this questioning playwright, the world becomes endlessly ironic. Whenever a seeking character seems to find a frame of reference for life, he discovers a larger context that mocks his limited vision. His impulses, his ideals, his facts, even his self often turn out to be illusory, or relative. This incisive, incessant questioning is often brilliantly done; but, incessant as it is, it raises a further question that brings us to the second part of our equation: from what stance do all these questions come? Is there any center? Any focus? Is there any meaning in this questioning of meaning?

Pirandello has been called a pessimist. Well, an artist is entitled to pessimism if, seeing something of the wholeness of life, with some soundness, he can find only despair in it; if his pessimism is the voice of a spirit that has plumbed experience selflessly, and must cry out a dark truth. The playwright is certainly not obligated to use drama to preach hope: Pirandello wrote justly to his actress friend Marta Abba, "Since art belongs to the realm of disinterested feeling, one must choose between the objectives of art and those of propaganda. The two cannot be practiced together." But: "disinterested feeling." Could this artist really function as an impersonal prism, focussing the drama of life onto the stage without any personal bias? Pirandello seemed to feel he had achieved such a neutral, refractive method: interviewed in London, he reiterated his favorite description of his technique:

> I have had the audacity of placing a mirror in the very center of the stage. It is the mirror of intelligence. Man, while alive, lives but does not see himself. Sentiment, by itself, is blind; I have therefore so managed that this blind man at a certain moment should open his eyes and should see himself in that mirror and should stand as if frozen by the unthought-of image of his own life.

But Pirandello's way of "reflecting" life, as he noted in his *Six Characters* preface, was to let his characters act out his own torments. Is he holding the mirror up to himself? Then how disinterested is his own response to life? Do his personal involvements affect the truth of what he sees in his looking glass?

Particularly revealing here are Pirandello's occasional affirmations. They seem to have no real place in the dark mirror into which he is staring, but rather to be dragged in as a deliberate attempt to lighten the gloom. Even so, he does not exploit those usual symbolic triumphs of fertility over decay, love and marriage; in Pirandello these are almost always insubstantial, usually lost in irony, turning out to be products of illusion, or passing impulse, or social pressure, or of destructive passion. When Pirandello brings himself to think positively, he reaches for miraculous assurance beyond the savage reflections of life he normally recognizes. And, inevitably, as even Vittorini, the playwright's over-fond champion observes, the more Pirandello tries to deal with constructive thought, the poorer his play. (...)

In *Tonight We Improvise*, another play that laughs at the theater's shortcomings in the face of art, the playwright's personal motif is even more clearly stated. In this play involving an acting company about to put on a Pirandello play, the actors— except when drawn into the story of the "eternal" characters— are all stereotypes of vanity and superficiality, directed by the bumbling, loquacious Dr. Hinkfuss. Hinkfuss, in his extended philosophical monologues to the audience, often speaks Pirandello's central philosophy. He argues that every man tries to create a timeless self, but must fail, because the self is transient, utilitarian, and always in danger of being "thwarted, perverted, and deformed" by life. What Hinkfuss then says is most revealing of Pirandello's own view: "Art, in a certain sense, is a revenge on life." *Revenge on life*—this sounds a theme that echoes again in Pirandello's drama—and also in his personal correspondence, as we shall see. Thus, in *As You Desire Me*, the Unknown One, deriding Salter's claims to being a serious writer, offers this proof—that he never had "felt compelled—because of a real torment, a real despair—to take *revenge on life* as it is, as it has been made for you by other people and through circumstances...." The verb in both cases is *vendicare*, which means revenge in the strongest sense—getting even for an offense suffered. One who thinks often of revenge is *vendicativo*-revengeful.

Much of Pirandello's drama, it begins to appear, has been a revenge on life—and on the theater and its audience, which never, it seemed to him, fully appreciated his excellence. Well, they would be sorry. In naked letters to Marta Abba, recently published, he complained bitterly of Italy's failure to accept his ideas for a national theater, Italy's failure to applaud all his work. Of the unfavorable reception of *Lazarus*, he cried out, with adolescent self-pity:

> What can I do about it? I cannot think of anything I have done to bring out this ill-feeling against me. I have worked. In one year I contributed four plays to the dramatic literature of my country. Time will tell if they are alive and vital: they will survive. And my country will have to live down the shame of having misunderstood them and of having treated me unjustly. But by now I am used to being insulted and it no longer hurts me.

When *Tonight We Improvise* opened in Berlin, part of the audience was violently against it—"the black envy of a gang of rascals, egged on by my ex-translator." Pirandello reports that most Germans thought the play wonderful; but he broods, sees himself the enduring, misunderstood hero:

> You see how right I had been to feel worried.... Last night I thought I was back in Italy. Everywhere I am pursued by hatred. Perhaps it is only right that this should be so, that I should die this way, annihilated by the hatred of triumphant cowards, by the incomprehension of idiots. After all they are the majority. The catcalls of idiots and of my enemies would not hurt me if my spirit were still what it used to be. But I have lost the pride of my isolation, the love of my disconsolate sadness.... My two staring eyes remain inexorably fixed, despairing, proud, tired, heavy-lidded with a pain that no one

will ever be able to understand or know. A great absolute immobility.

To the end of his life he was working out his revenge on a world that treated him so. In his last year, he wrote Marta Abba, "Mankind does not deserve anything, stubborn as it is in its constantly growing stupidity, in its brutal quarrelsomeness."

—Marvin Rosenberg, "Pirandello's Mirror," *Modernism in European Drama: Ibsen, Strindberg, Pirandello, Beckett. Essays From Modern Drama*, eds. Frederick J. Marker and Christopher Innes (University of Toronto Press, 1988): 127–41.

WORKS BY
Luigi Pirandello

(dates and translations are necessarily approximate)

L'Esclusa (*The Outcast*), 1893.

La Morsa (under title *L'epilogo*), 1898.

Il Turno (*The Merry-Go-Raound of Love*), 1902.

Il fu Mattia Pascal (*The Late Mattia Pascal*), 1904.

Lumie di Sicilia, 1911.

Il dovere del medico, 1912.

I vecchi e i giovani (*The Young and the Old*), 1913.

Liola, 1917.

Pensaci, Giacomino! (*Think, Giacomino!*), 1917.

Il berretto a sonagli (*Cap and Bells*), 1917.

Così è (se vi pare), [*Right You Are (If You Think You Are)*], 1918.

Il piacere dell'onesta (*The Pleasure of Honesty*), 1918.

La patente, 1918.

Ma non e una cosa seria, 1919.

Il giuoco delle parti (*The Rules of the Game*), 1919.

Tutto per bene (*All for the Best*), 1920.

La ragione degli altri, 1921.

Come prima, meglio di prima, 1921.

L'innesto, 1921.

Sei personaggi in cerca d'autore (*Six Characters in Search of an Author*) 1921.

Enrico IV, 1922.

La signora Morli, una e due, 1922.

Vestire gli ignudi (*To Dress the Naked*), 1922.

L'uomo, la bestia, e la virtu (*The Man with the Flower in his Mouth*), 1923.

La vita che ti diedi (*The Life I Gave You*), 1923.

Ciascuno a suo modo (*Each in his Own Way*), 1924.

La giara, 1925.

L'altro figlio, 1925.

Sagra del Signore della Nave, 1925.

Cece, 1926.

All'uscita, 1926.

L'imbecille, 1926.

L'uomo dal fiore in bocca, 1926.

Diana e la Tuda (*Diana and Tuda*), 1926.

Bellavita, 1927.

L'amica delle mogli (*The Wives' Friend*), 1927.

La nuova colonia (*The New Colony*), 1928.

O di uno o di nessuno, 1929.

Lazzaro (*Lazarus*), 1929.

Questa sera si recita a soggetto (*Tonight We Improvise*), 1929.

Come tu mi vuoi (*As You Desire Me*) 1930.

Trovarsi (*To find Oneself*), 1932.

Quando si e qualcuno (*When One is Somebody*), 1933.

Non si sa come (*No One Knows How*), 1935.

Sogno (ma forse no), 1936.

I giganti della montagna (*The Mountain Giants*), 1937.

La favola del figlio cambiato, 1938.

WORKS ABOUT
Luigi Pirandello

Andersson, G. *Arte e teoria: Studi sulla poetica del giovane Luigi Pirandello*. Stockholm: Almquisst and Wikell, 1966.

Bassnett, Susan. *Luigi Pirandello*. London: MacMillan, 1983.

———, ed. *File on Pirandello*. London, 1989.

———and Jennifer Lorch, eds. *Luigi Pirandello in the Theatre: a Documentary Record*. Philadelphia: Harwood Academic Publishers, 1993.

Bentley, Eric. *The Playwright as Thinker: A Study of Drama in Modern Times*. 8th ed. Cleveland and New York, 1963.

———. *The Pirandello Commentaries*. Evanston: Northwestern Univ. Press, 1986.

Bishop, Tom. *Pirandello and the French Theatre*. London, 1960.

Bloom, Harold. Ed., *Luigi Pirandello, Modern Critical Views*. Chelsea House Publishers, 1989.

Bragaglia, Leonardo. *Interpreti Pirandelliani*. Rome: Trevi, 1969.

Budel, Oscar. *Pirandello*. London, 1966.

Cambon, Glauco, ed. *Pirandello, a Collection of Critical Essays*, in the series *Twentieth Century Views*. Englewood Cliffs, New Jersey, 1967.

Caputi, Anthony Francis. *Pirandello and the Crisis of Modern Consciousness*. Urbana: Univ. of Ill. Press, 1988.

Coveney, Michael. *The Aisle Is Full of Noises*. London: Nick Hern, 1994.

Croce, Benedetto. "Luigi Pirandello." *La Letteratura Italiana*. Vol. 4. Pari: Laterza, 1963.

DiGaetani, J.L. (ed.) *A Companion to Pirandello Studies*. Greenwood Press, 1991.

Dombroski, Robt. S. *Le totalita dell'artificio: ideologia e forme nel romanzo di Pirandello*. Padova: Liviana, 1978.

Ferrante, L. *Luigi Pirandello*. Florence, 1958.

Fisher, James. *The Theatre of Yesterday and Tomorrow: commedia dell'arte on the Modern Stage*. Lewiston: E. Mellen Press, 1992.

Gilman, Richard. *The Making of Modern Drama: a study of Buchner, Ibsen, Strindberg, Chekhov, Pirandello, Brecht, Beckett, Handke*. New York: Farrar, Straus and Giroux, 1974.

Giudice, Gaspare. *Pirandello: A Biography*. Trans. A. Hamilton. London: Oxford University Press, 1975.

Gruber, Wm. E. *Missing Persons: Character and Characterization in Modern Drama*. Athens, GA: University of GA Press, 1994.

Gunsberg, Maggie. *Gender and the Italian Stage: From the Renaissance to the Present Day*. Cambridge University Press, 1997.

—————. *Patriarchal Representations: Gender and Discourse in Pirandello's Theatre*. Oxford: Berg, 1994.

Kennedy, Andrew K. *Six Dramatists in Search of a Language: Studies in Dramatic Literature*. London: Cambridge University Press, 1975.

Lauretta, Enzo, ed. *La trilogia di Pirandello*. National Center of Pirandellani Studies, Agrigento, 1977.

MacClintock, L. *The Age of Pirandello*. Indiana University Press, 1951.

Mariani, Umberto. *La creasione del vero: il maggior teatro di Pirandello*. Fiesole: Cadmo, 2001.

Nardelli, Federico V. *Vita segreta di Luigi Pirandello*. Rome: V. Bianco, 1962.

Nelson, Robert J. *Play within a Play*. New Haven: Yale University Press, 1959.

Newberry, Wilma. *The Pirandellian Mode in Spanish Literature*. Albany, NY: SUNY Press, 1973.

Oliver, Roger W. *Dreams of Passion: The Theater of Luigi Pirandello*. Gotham Library of NY Univ. Press, 1979.

Paolucci, Anne. *Pirandello's Theater, the Recovery of the Modern Stage for Dramatic Art*. Carbondale: Southern Illinois University Press, 1974.

Ragusa, Olga. *Luigi Pirandello*. New York: Columbia Univ. Press, 1968.

—————. *Luigi Pirandello: an approach to his theatre*. Edinburgh: Edinburgh University Press, 1980.

Rauhut, Franz. *Der Junge Pirandello*. Munich, 1964.

Starkie, Walter. *Luigi Pirandello*. University of California Press, 1965 (first pub. 1926).

Stone, Jennifer. *Pirandello's Naked Prompt: The Structure of Repetition in Modernism*. Ravenna: Longo, 1989.

Vincentini, C. *L'estetica di Pirandello*. Milan: Mursia, 1970.

Valency, Maurice. *The End of the World: An Introduction to Contemporary Drama*. Oxford: University Press, 1980.

Vittorini, Domenico. *The Drama of Luigi Pirandello*. New York, 1957 (first pub. 1935.

Witt, Mary Ann Frese. *The Search for Modern Tragedy: aesthetic fascism in Italy and France*. Ithaca: Cornell University Press, 2001.

ACKNOWLEDGMENTS

"Pirandello's *Six Characters* and Surrealism" by Anna Balakian from *A Companion to Pirandello Studies*, Ed. John Louis DiGaetani. © 1991 by Greenwood Press. Reprinted by permission.

"Henry IV—The Tragic Humorist" by Susan Bassnett from *A Companion to Pirandello Studies*. © 1991 by Greenwood Press. Reprinted by permission.

Luigi Pirandello by Susan Bassnett-McGuire. © 1983 by Grove Press. Reprinted by permission.

"*Enrico IV*: The Tragic Emperor" by Eric Bentley from *Tulane Drame Review* 10, 3 (Spring 1966). © 1966 by *Tulane Drama Review*. Reprinted by permission.

Haskell M. Block, "Some Notes on the Problem of Modern Tragedy" from *Comparative Literature Studies* 9, 1. (University Park: The Penn State University Press): pp. 80–84. © 1972 Penn State University Press. Reprinted by permission of the publisher.

Reprinted from *Characters and Authors in Luigi Pirandello* by Ann Hallamore Caesar (1998) by permission of Oxford University Press. © 1988 by Ann Hallamore Caesar.

"The Theatrical Matrix of Experience" by Anthony Caputi from *Pirandello and the Crisis of Modern Consciousness*. © 1988 by the Board of Trustees of the University of Illinois. Used with permission of the University of Illinois Press.

"Pirandello's Notion of Time" by Luisetta Chomel from *Canadian Journal of Italian Studies* 12. © 1989 by Luisetta Chomel. Reprinted by permission.

"Henry IV and Time" by Anthony DeVivo from *Canadian Journal of Italian Studies* 12. © 1989 by Anthony DeVivo. Reprinted by permission.

"Adultery: The Paternal Potential" by Ursula Fanning from *Yearbook of the Society for Pirandello Studies* 15. © 1995–1996 by Ursula Fanning. Reprinted by permission.

Themes and Ideas